ICONIC MELBOURNE

A u s t r a l i a

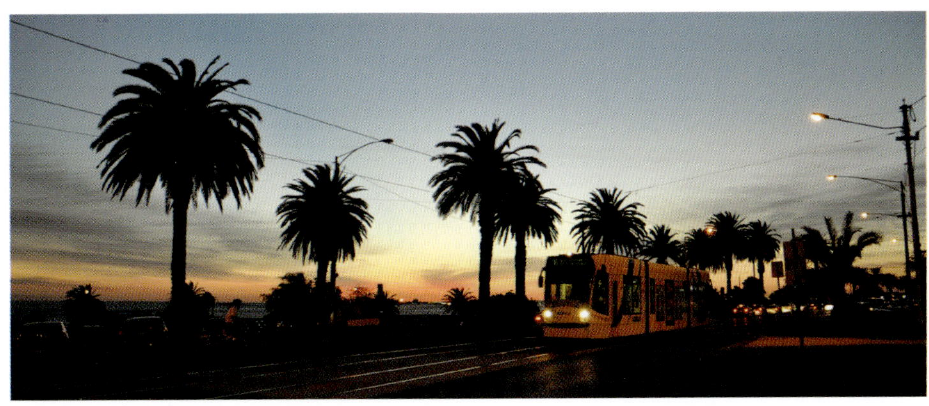

All Original Paintings, Photography and Poetry by Melbourne Artist **Mark Rusic**

"Energy bursts out from inside of me as I work as an artist, poet and photographer, especially when harnessing the strength of all three mediums to create an art-unison.

Applying this passion to my wonderful city of Melbourne, where I grew up, has brought an immense degree of personal fulfilment. I feel called to craft meaningful, quality art that literally gives joy, and shows the world at new angles. My task also involves encouraging people to reach their full creative potential whether as a hobbyist- or involved in the arts, design, literary, media, entertainment or business spheres, while also using their artistry as a powerful medium to inspire a positive social outlook. My broader vision is to go beyond Melbourne city to other iconic cities of the world and create books inspired by the landmarks that define each place, using this three-pronged creative approach—of inspiring memories, sharing the city's history, while providing an enriching vicarious experience through the visual and literary forms of painting, poetry and photography."

MARK RUSIC

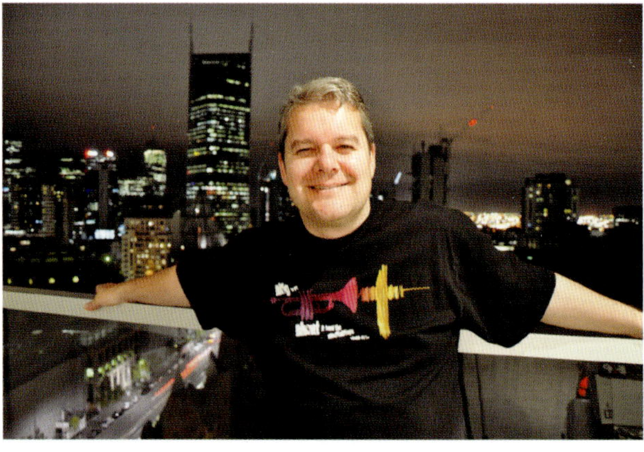

Wholesale Enquiries:

Phone: +61 430066793

Email: givejoydesigns@gmail.com

ISBN:978-0-646-91172-4

Front Cover - Flinders St Station, Melbourne

Back Cover - MCG, Melbourne & testimonials

All Original Paintings, Poetry & Photography By Mark Rusic

Designed in Australia by Mark Rusic Publishing

Iconic Melbourne showcases more than 20 of Melbourne's finest locations utilising Artist, Mark Rusic's, own original collection of paintings, poetry and photography, to present Melbourne in this very fresh, dynamic and unique publication. The iconic locations include: MCG, Federation Square and the Old Melbourne Gaol to name a few.

What sets *Iconic Melbourne* apart is not only how we learn about and celebrate each icon, but how the artist uses his artistry to create a kind of 'iconic-impetus' to also encourage a positive social outlook, while inspiring the reader to discover and be empowered in their own creative potential.

Firstly, the paintings help the reader to encounter the warmth and beauty of the various landmarks. The artist also shares some personal thoughts about his painting technique, and about painting in general. The poetry is used to question the icons and what they represent while at the same time, to celebrate their tangible form in Melbourne City's landscape. The photography reveals certain key features of the poem, so the meaning becomes more impressionable.

So, using all three media in their combined strength this presentation of Melbourne is second to none. In many ways, this book can become a very personal and vicarious experience; both a pleasurable and thought provoking part of your life journey.

This book will be a tremendous gift and memory for you, your friends and family. Enjoy!

You will not be alone in valuing Mark's work. Here are some testimonials from buyers in Melbourne, and from various places across the globe. (See the back cover for more.)

"Love the colour-Melbourne the way it is!" **(Melbourne)**

"Amazing colours, brilliant memories for us to take home." **(UK)**

"Beautiful colours and vibrant to the eye. Great artwork." **(Chicago)**

"Give you joy designs. Fantastic pictures." **(Noosa QLD)**

"Colour Colour Colour! Great images will look fantastic on my walls." **(Brisbane)**

"We like the unusualness, colour and creativity." **(Melbourne)**

"Thanks so much-the picture of the MCG perfectly captures the energy and beauty we found throughout Australia." **(England)**

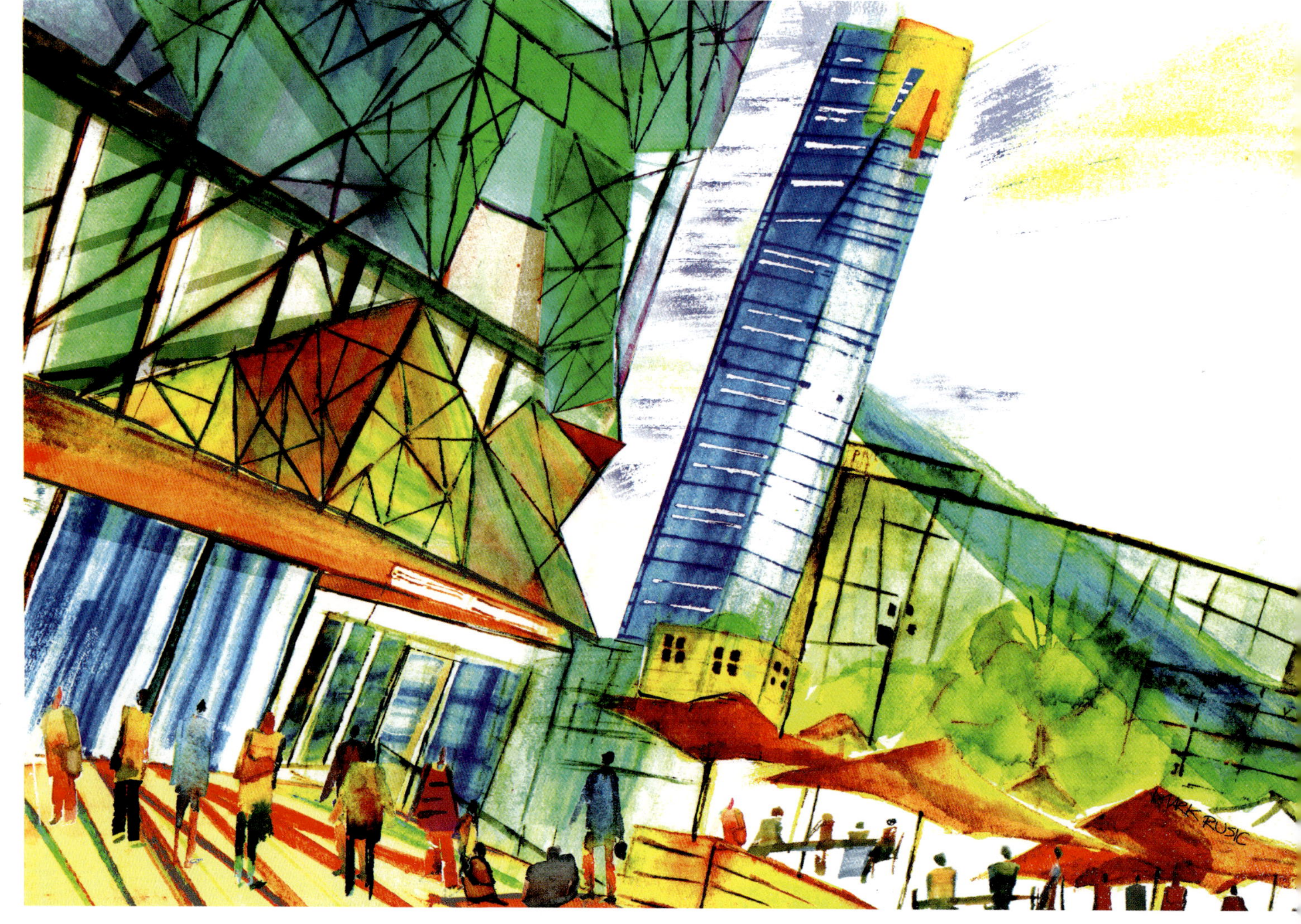
MARK RUSIC

Federation Square

A longing for identity. A longing to be one.
A longing to be Australian began the movement for federation
1901 the trans-formation began, each colony wanting its own.
Eventually all agreed, better off as a nation, than going it alone.

Australians began to celebrate in poems and in songs,
with improvement in transport and communication
soon arose a mighty throng. One hundred years later
a prime monument to the partnership was made.
In a place where the people can gather as one—Federation Square
May this spirit never fade.

The construction was not without its baptism of fire, years overtime
Many argued her appearance was marred
Much concern about the height and placement of those shards!
Budgets blew out, design elements made tempers flare-
But today, people love it… It's been worth all the care.

Our City proclaims Federation with gratitude; an answer to prayer
The first seating of federal parliament was held
not far from the Square. It is a place of legacy
in more ways than one. A symbol of a coming together,
of a nation, our leaders in unison.

Painting *Federation Square with Eureka Tower, Southgate* [Left]
I laboured over those triangular shapes though I'm sure it was nothing compared to the original construction!

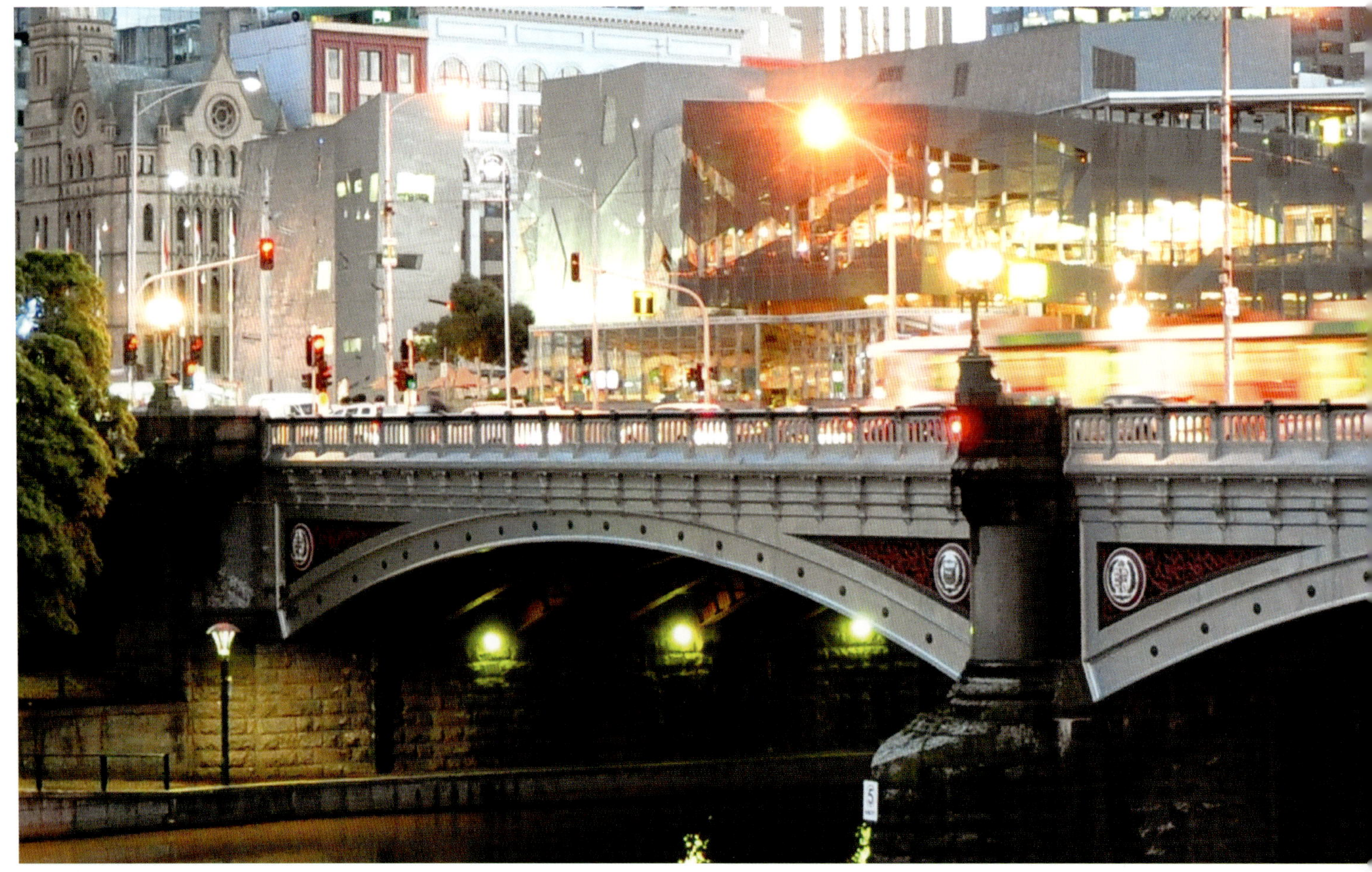

Photo *Federation Square adjacent Yarra Bridge* [Above]

Here is Federation Square experiencing the 'baptism of fire' mentioned in the poem. Notice how I am using the lighting effects to achieve this imagery of fire.

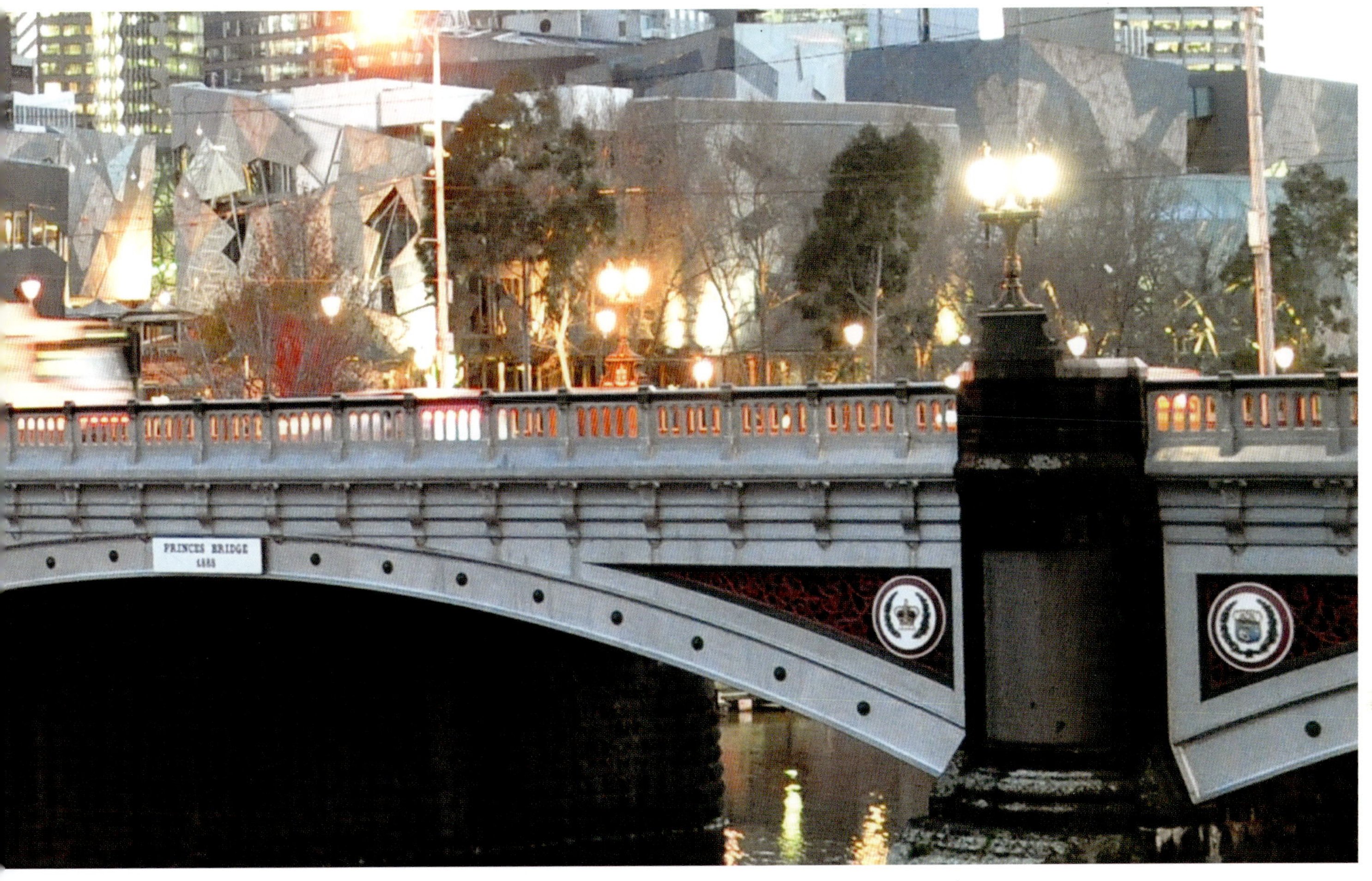
PRINCES BRIDGE

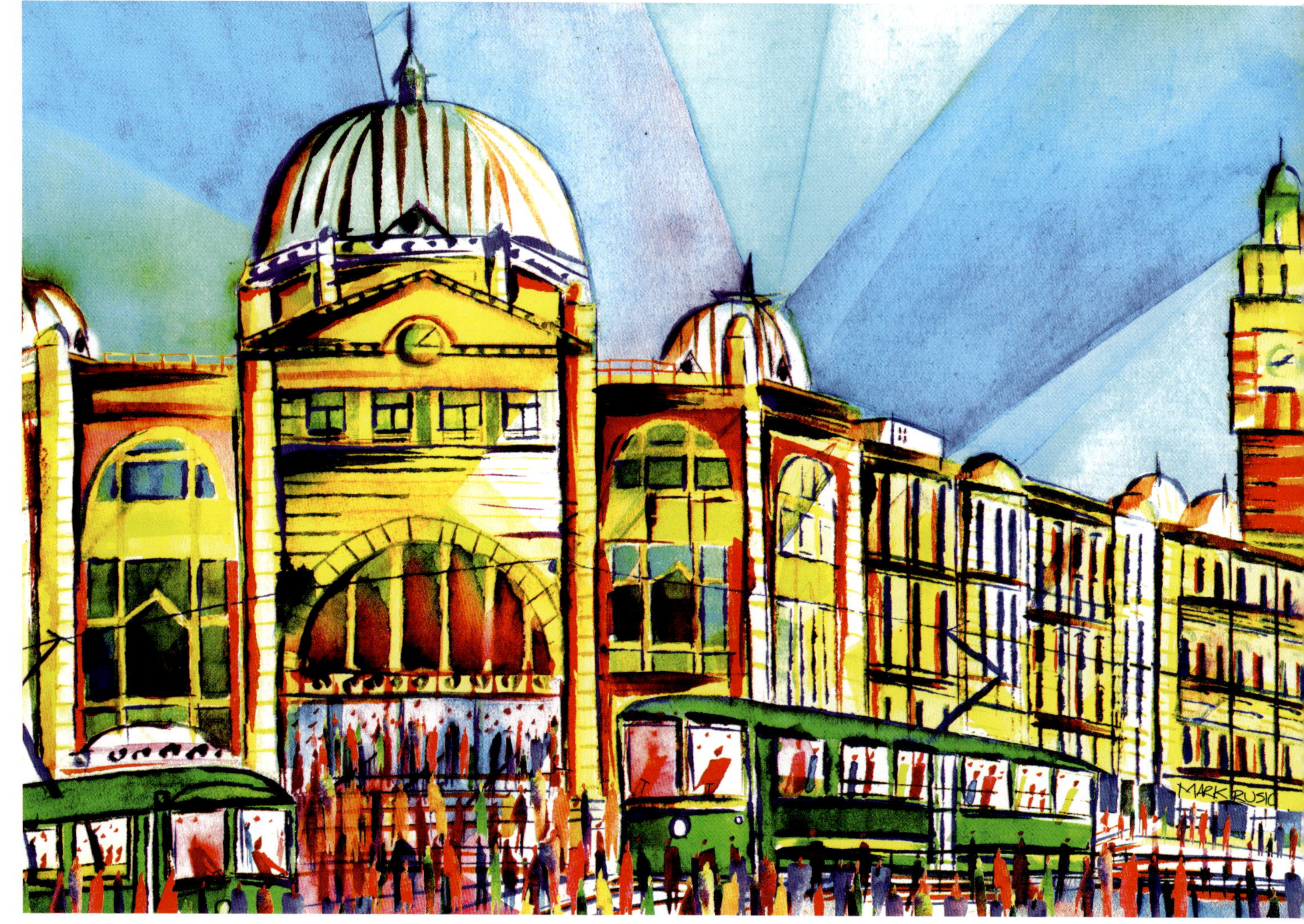
MARK RUSIC

Flinders Street Station

Flinders Street Station ahead. Can't wait to see The Clocks.
Friday night, home-time. To the entrance, everyone flocks.
myki card zipped. In and out of the slot. Walk under the big green dome
Darting past the entry gates. One step closer to home.

In the rush, a scarf is dropped. Race ahead. Pass it to them.
In a gesture, a small kindness. They see in you a friend. Not foe.

Down the escalator. Some fighting to be first.
Better not jump the queue... patience is a virtue.
Don't want someone to curse!

On the crowded platform. Whistles. Chugs. Cancellations. Check
arrival time. A little reading or music. Why not something new: write a rhyme?
A sea of iPads appear. On the net they surf.
For a moment, glance at others. Stalking
that ideal seat. That's my turf!

In another moment imagine
feeling free to chat. People sitting across from you. Hearty conversations.
No strangers in silence. Wouldn't it be nice to share your day,
your thoughts. If only we were...

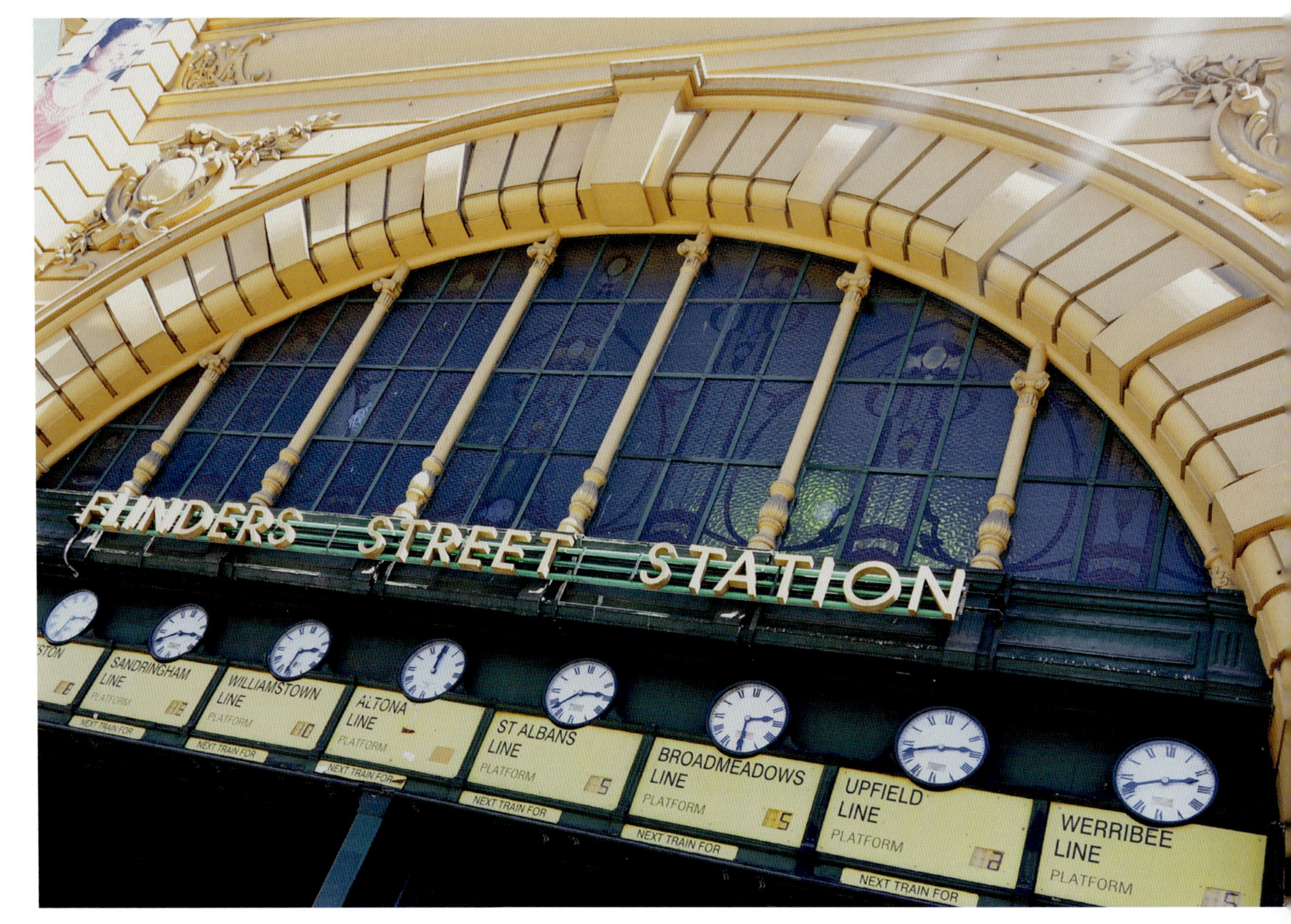

FLINDERS STREET STATION
SANDRINGHAM LINE
PLATFORM
NEXT TRAIN FOR
WILLIAMSTOWN LINE
PLATFORM
NEXT TRAIN FOR
ALTONA LINE
PLATFORM
NEXT TRAIN FOR
ST ALBANS LINE
PLATFORM
NEXT TRAIN FOR
BROADMEADOWS LINE
PLATFORM
NEXT TRAIN FOR
UPFIELD LINE
PLATFORM
NEXT TRAIN FOR
WERRIBEE LINE
PLATFORM

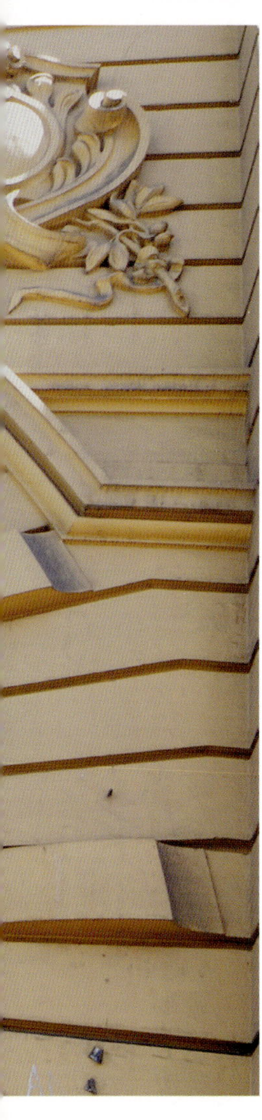

Flinders Street Station *continued...*

...Train arrives. Onward we go. Homeward bound.
Family time. Friends drop in. Mum cooking up a storm.
Brothers and sisters can't wait to see me, share the day.
This is my heart's longing for all families: that *This* can be the norm

Trains rattle, bump along the line. Thoughts drift to the clutter on the carriage...
To thoughts of family life. How do I improve mine? Clean up the clutter.
Get back to the important things of life. Invest in my family. Enjoy them.
Include them. Show meaningful, little gestures—a quick call to say I care—a gift that says *I love you*.
Big hugs. Quality time. It need not be rare.

Painting *Flinders Street Station* [Previous page]
One person I met commented on buying artwork generally: 'It's not that I don't want to buy any artwork, it's just that I can't find anything worth buying and actually putting on my walls.' The challenge to the artist and designer is to deliver artwork with a compelling degree of freshness and originality in a world gone 'copy and imitation' mad! I was thrilled that he bought my painting.

Photo *Flinders Street Station Clocks* [Left]
This is arguably the most prominent cultural icon of Melbourne. The station and facade was actually completed in 1909. A common Melbourne idiom is to say: 'I'll meet you under the clocks.' Multitudes of people pass under them daily to arrive in the city, or journey home to family.

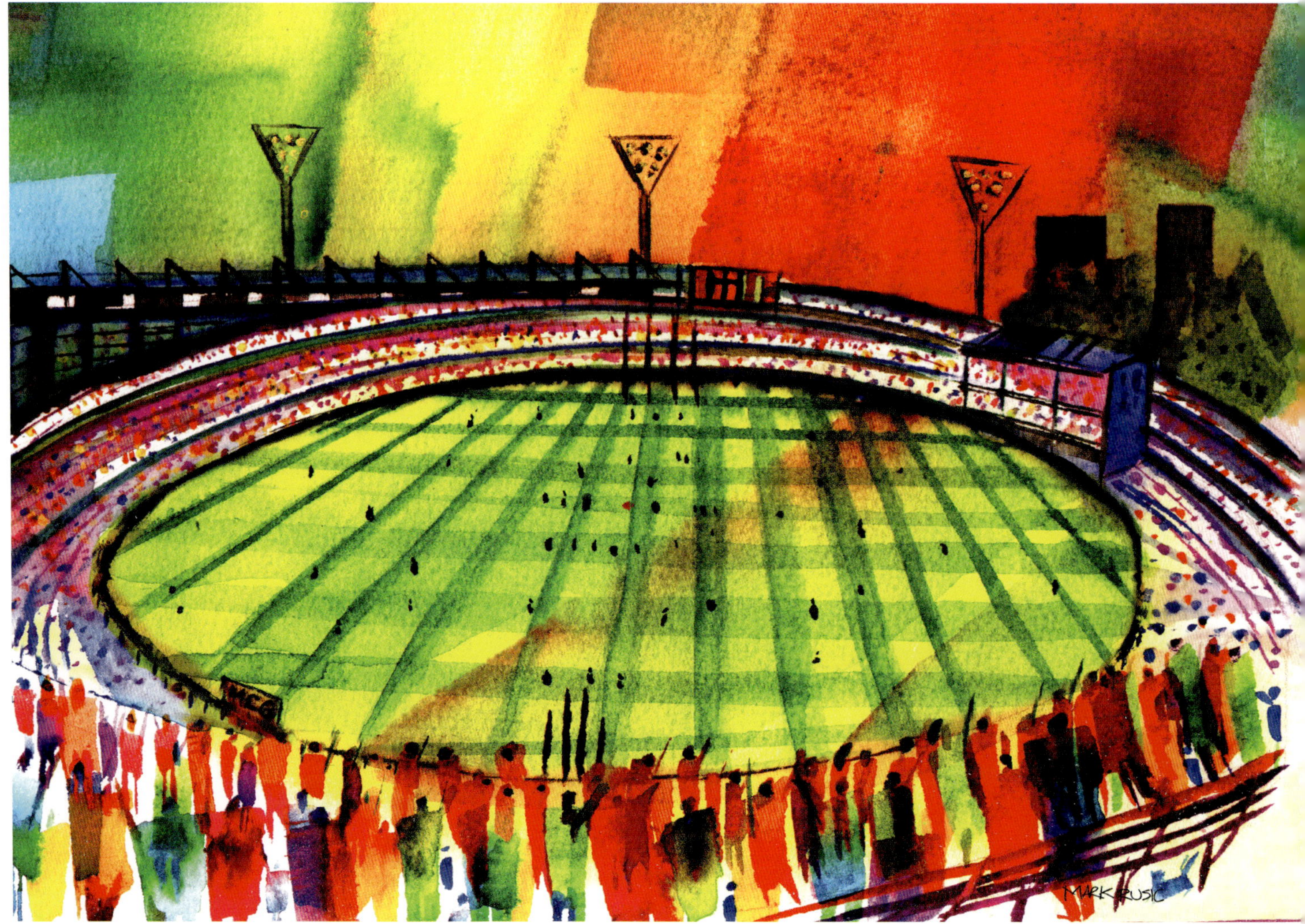
MARK RUSIC

Melbourne Cricket Ground

We treasure the *G*. People say it's a must: *I've got to go*.
See the towering lights from afar. Like marching ants
they come. Can't wait to be front row!
Multitudes wave banners
and fists as the players soar. A mark taken. Wickets tumble.
Atmosphere electric. The crowd ROARS!

We treasure the *G*. We love our heroes of sport.
From each generation are there many, and never naught.
Great women and men whose legacy
we remember… Their class of excellence, of style, of attitude. And more.
Great names inscribed upon the walls. And kids collecting and swapping
Footy cards galore!

I want to say: Heroes don't come easy. Appreciate those on field.
Not all can be *top of the ladder*. Costs are Huge—personal life, personal rights
All yield.
Expectations keep rising. Competition takes its toll.
Will sportsmanship continue the focus. Or is it me, myself and I: the soul?

May many new heroes arise. Can break out like a storm. Come diamond
from the charcoal—Intense heat and pressure; great investment before transformed.
So, keep encouraging our players to
maximise the talent they wield
May their lives glisten like diamonds, be stellar examples
on and off the field.

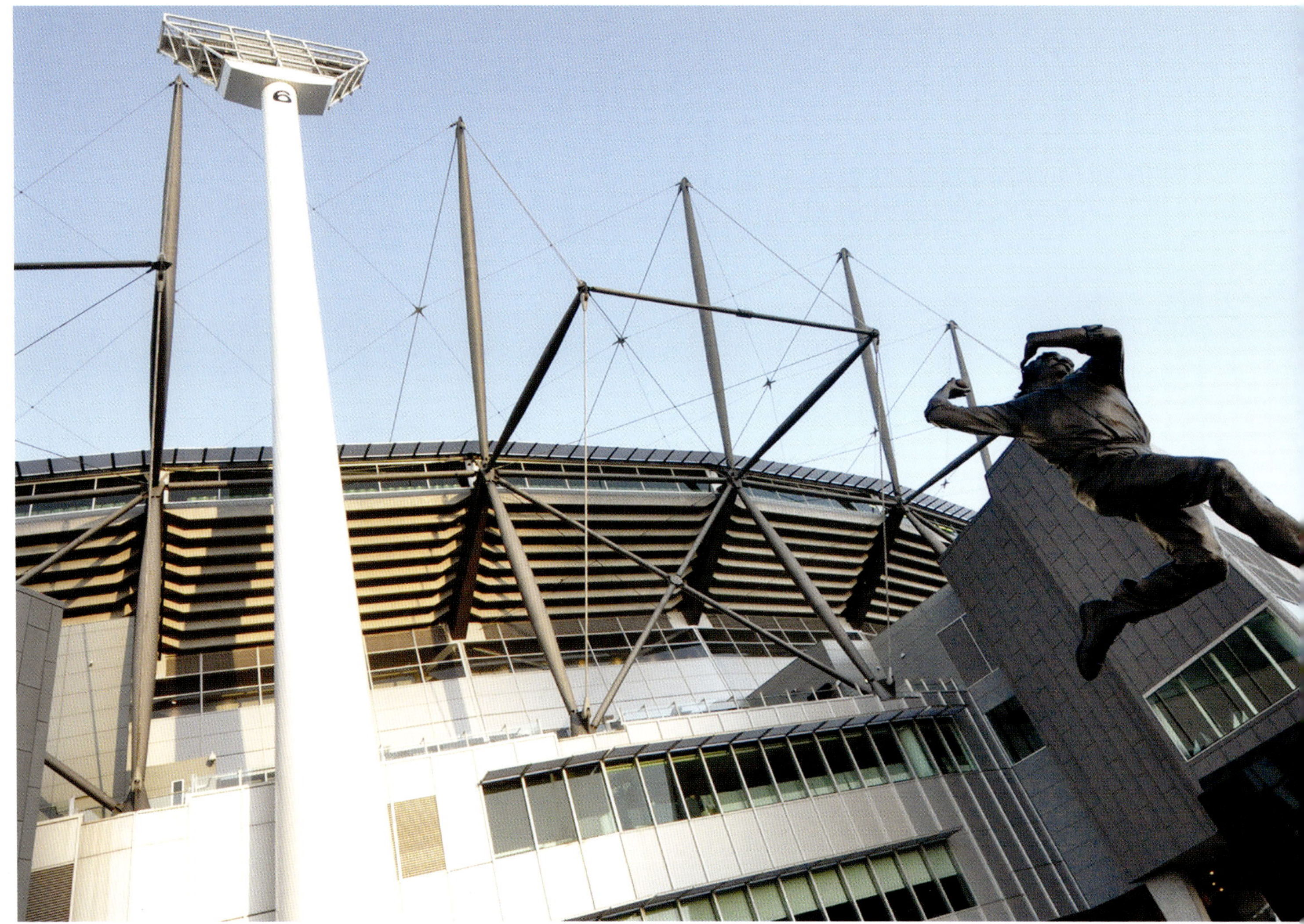
6

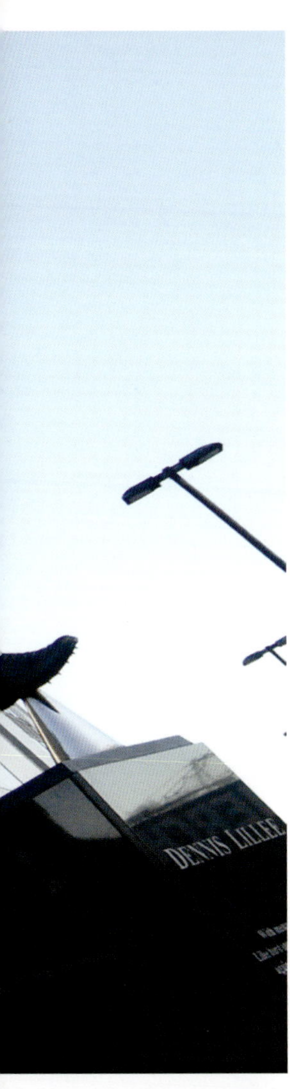

Painting *Melbourne Cricket Ground* [Previous page]
When I thought of painting the MCG I had one main thing in mind. In my mind's eye I was constantly focused on the lovely greens you see on the ground. Painting it was divine!

Photo *Pedestal of Denis Lillee, MCG* [Left]
You certainly get an incredibly dignified representation of our heroes of sport at the Melbourne Cricket Ground. Here is one of the many pedestals you will find in honour of those that made their mark.

Reflection Every game has a spectrum of excitement. When the ball goes out of bounds; boring. When there is a valiant sprint toward the goals and a player is tackled and loses possession; we feel the pain. When the ball goes repeatedly near the goals, almost scores; we scream out in anguish. Then, you have adrenaline-rush moments. At centre bounce, every team member is firing. The ball goes straight down the middle like lightning, sometimes scoring three goals in row, or six or even ten! That feeling is palpable.

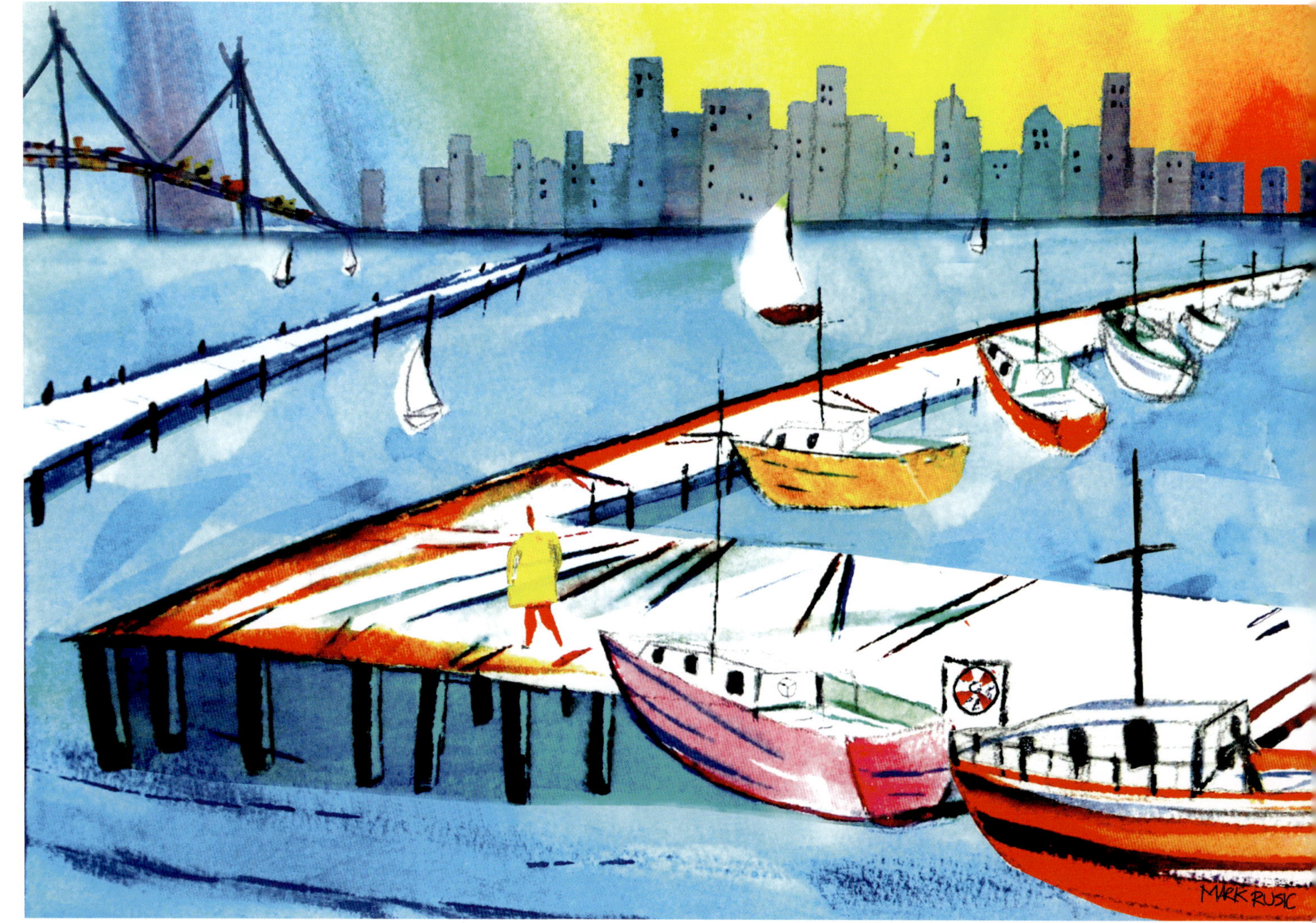
MARK RUSIC

Williamstown

Williamstown. A beautiful place. A wonderful shore.
Home for pelicans and black swans
fantastic city skyline views
a myriad of colourful boats
tiny
anchored down, moored to piers
dotted over the sea

What is the parallel in our daily lives?
Being moored is important. Friendship and accountability
define a life. Without mooring, people go adrift and off track.
Some people end up experiencing unnecessary strife.

Sometimes in life waves come in to pound us.
Thoughts of hopelessness and worries arise.
Thank God I am moored to a good community.
I am not battling alone to my demise.

By committing to community somewhere,
you grow when you show you care.

Some anchors are big. Others are small.
Just drop your anchor somewhere or
you can't be moored at all.

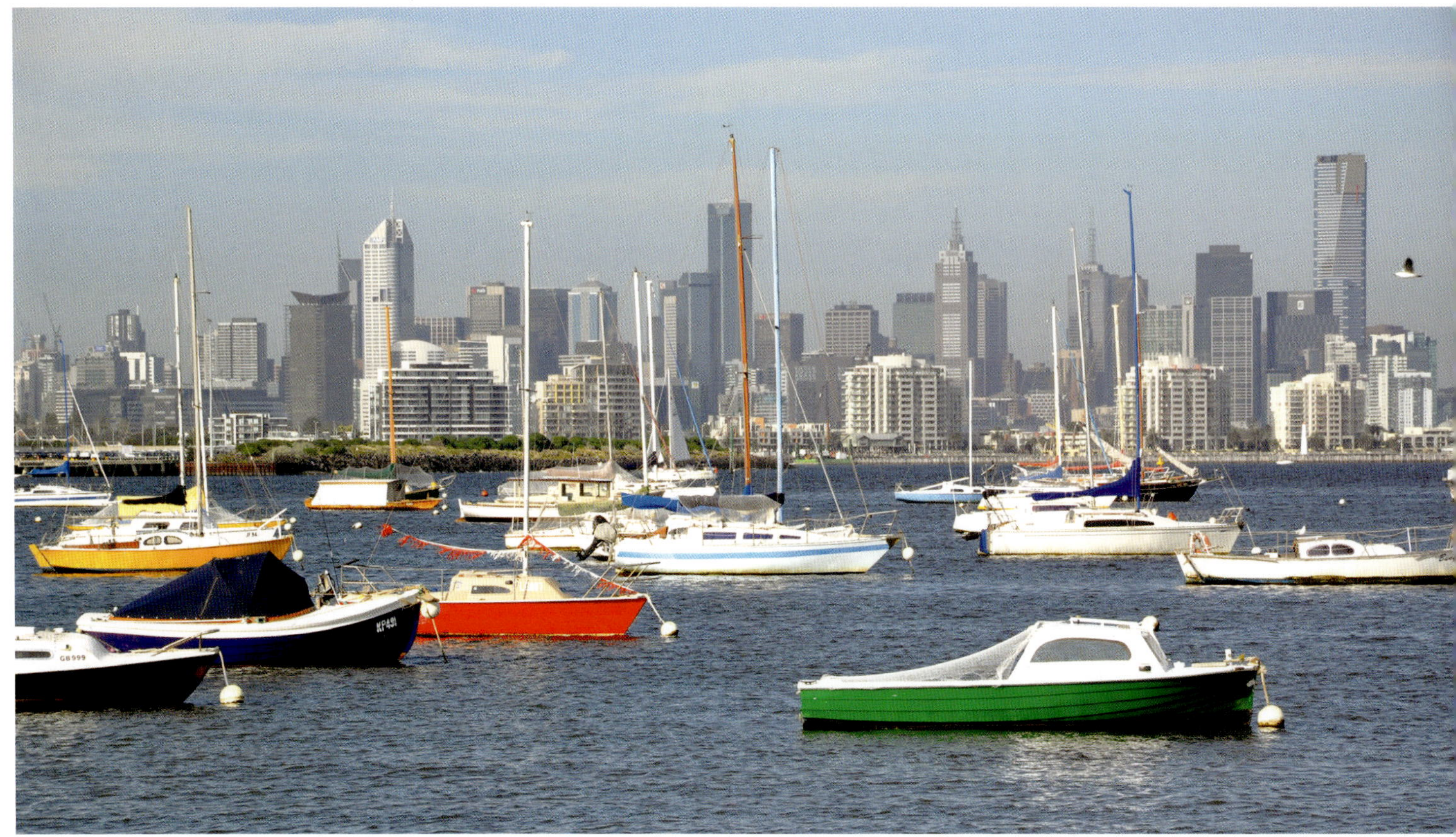

Painting — *Williamstown Foreshore* [Previous page]

Straight after I painted this, I sold many prints. No doubt, I think a lot of people like Williamstown and the views; the subject is popular. But, what I tried to do was to accentuate a few key features that count, and configure them all well. Aspects like the piers, the boats, the skyline; the blues of the sea were of crucial importance to make it eye-catching. I love this Williamtown view.

Tip — Think about it. Great paintings are actually often really, really simple. A major key to beauty and excellence is having the right composition. It involves configuring your selected features as one, with an optimum perspective. I am learning to do that.

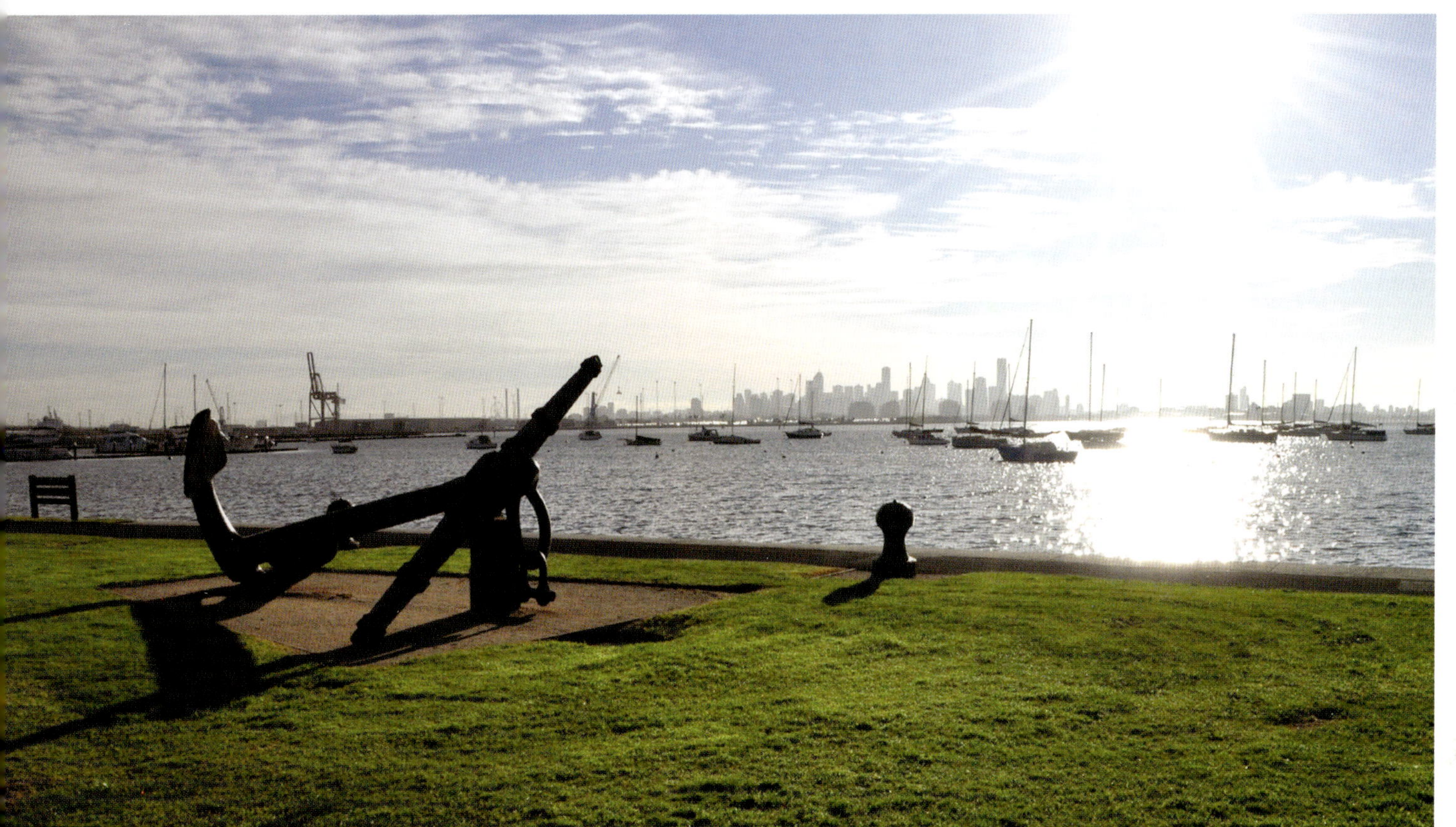

Photo *Boats along Williamstown Foreshore* [Left]
Captivating colours of the boats off the Williamstown shoreline.

Photo *Anchor Memorial, Williamstown Foreshore* [Above]
I managed to stumble upon this huge anchor which fitted the theme of being 'moored in life' really well.

Tip Taking photos facing the sun is photo-taboo in general. Understand why rules and taboos exist. But, realise you are not bound by such conditions. This kind of mindset enables originality to thrive.

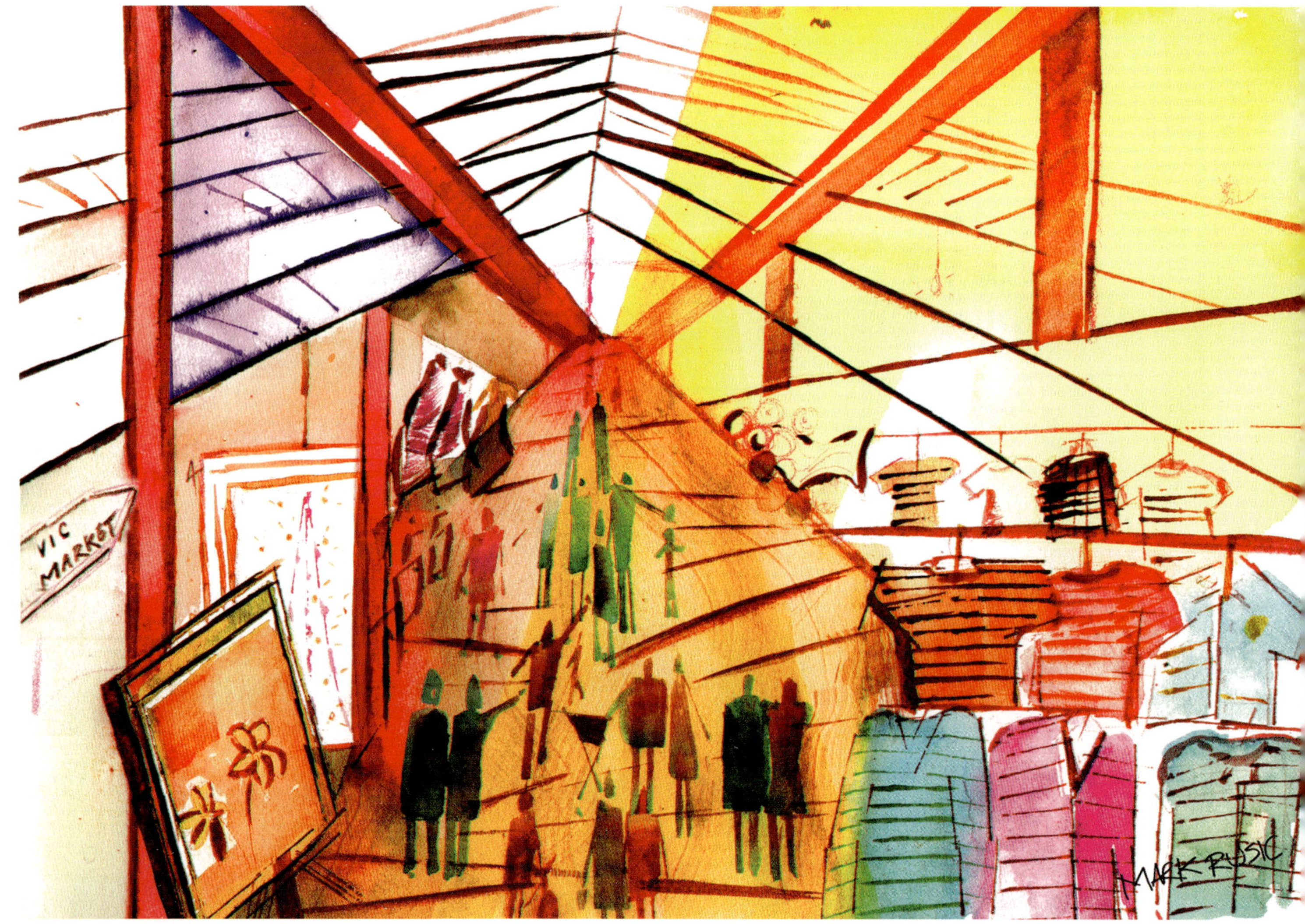
VIC MARKET
MARK RUSIC

Queen Victoria Market

Clothing, great eateries, souvenirs, people everywhere you see.
Smells, colours, fruits galore, plenty of variety.
Iconic facade with the bulls and ram above.
Tour the sheds. The fish markets and stalls you'll love.

Feel the breeze, the people rushing about
Those that relax, sit and eat in the sun
Where's the Ugg boots, the leather jackets?
Find them, while having fun.
There's something for everyone. Even ingredients and tinned cans.
Just when you thought you've seen it all,
watch the people queue up at the donut van.

Traders work hard, often arrive predawn to set up stall.
Enduring no matter what, winter freeze, summer fry-
more pleasant during autumn fall.
Traders call out, shouting as you pass by: will you agree their product is nice?
People appear disinterested, silently waiting for the right thing, at bargain price.

Traders are a community. They support each other through thick and thin.
Some have been there for 10, 15 years. Some die passing it on to next of kin.
It's wonderful to meet the older traders, solid like mighty oaks.
Lives rich in experience, so friendly, may God bless these folks.

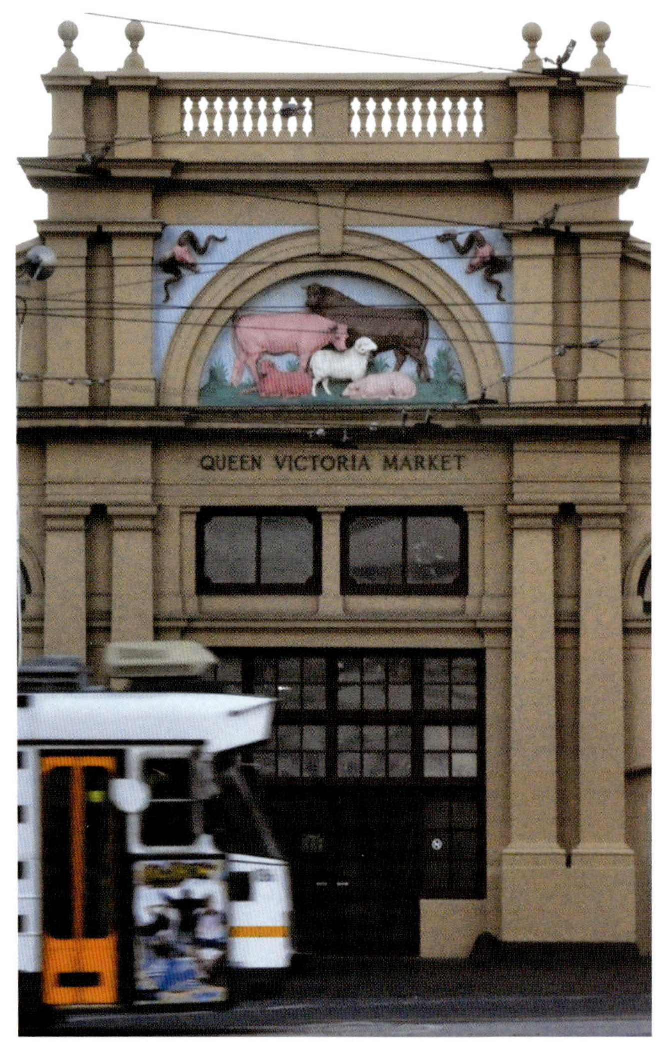
QUEEN VICTORIA MARKET

Queen Victoria Market *continued...*

So, if you're tired of the aircon-predictability of the malls
Come to the Queen Vic Market and expect to have a ball.
For more than 100 years, QV has been our cultural landmark
for tourists and locals alike. Her impact has been stark.

Painting *J-shed, Victoria Market* [Previous page]
I tried to use perspective to make the shed come alive. Some light enters the shed through the existing louvers. I distinctly drew this bright yellow to represent not just natural light, but the spirit of goodness entering the place. This was to bring refreshing encouragement to those working the stalls. Interestingly, straight after I painted it and put it up for sale, the stallholder next door bought it. His name was Bagus, which means 'good' in Indonesian. It felt like a kind of divine encounter.

Photo *Queen Victoria Market* [Left]
Iconic facade of the market entrance.

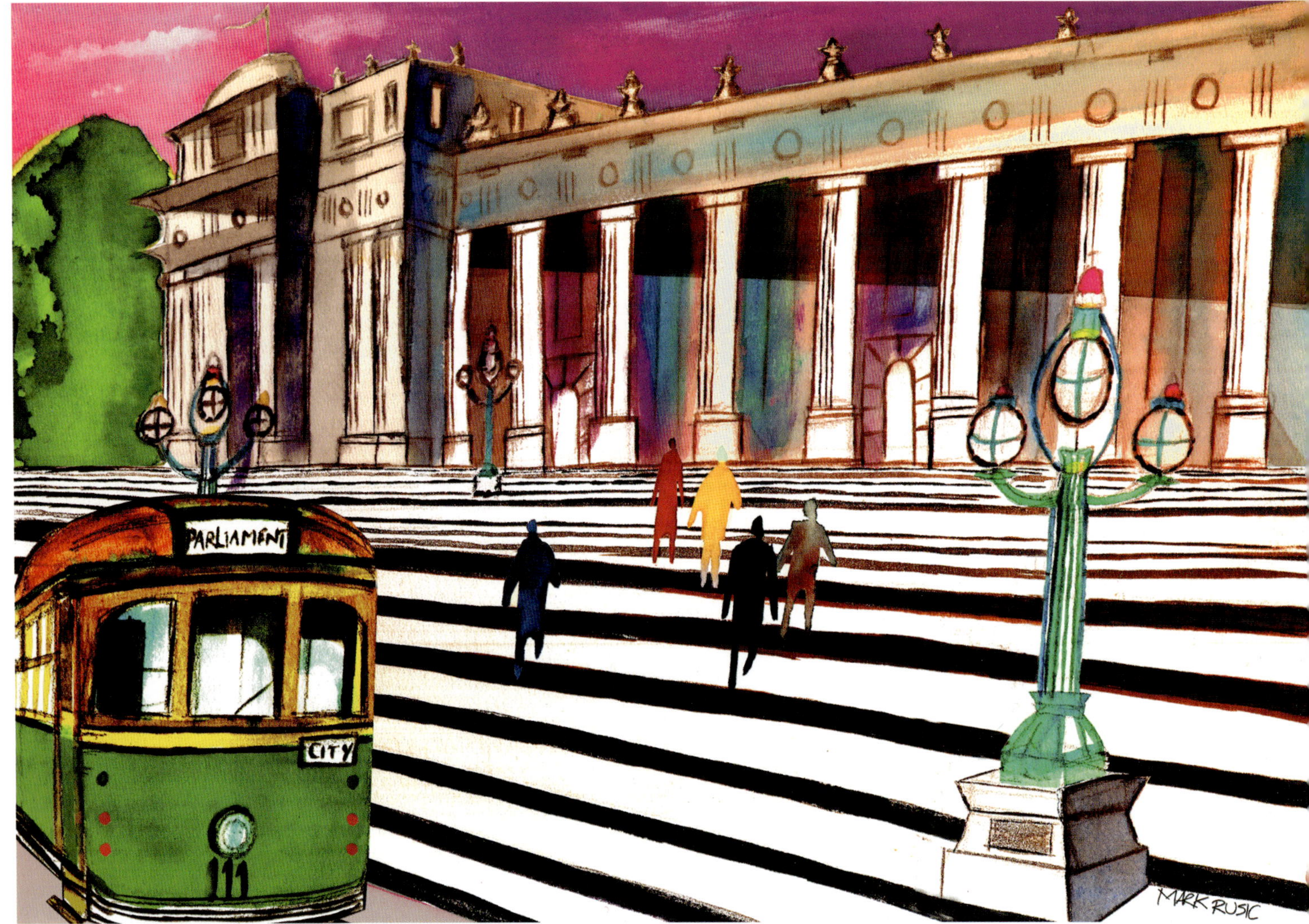
PARLIAMENT
CITY
111
MARK RUSIC

Parliament House

A great nation we have. Australia a great place to be.
Problems, compared to the world? Minimal—
such opportunity and free. We are so blessed.
Continue to develop our vision, leadership and strong
foundations. Lucky-country? Indefinitely—
Can't build on luck. How can Australia endure well the test of time?
Needless to say, to us all—
keep our heads down, work hard. Not too much wine!

Can we be more strategic in our nation's vision and planning?
Industries future: positioned to be strong. Not too hard to get things done
Business and enterprise rising
Nation with a renewed confidence; people with dreams a mighty throng.

Heart for refugees and the poor. Manage the economy well.
Truth is: How can we help others effectively, if our countries debt swells?

Continue to honour our leaders. Honour them from the heart.
Not enough thank-you mail. Too many protests. How can we ever make a good start?
What a difficult role to govern, to be a pillar in the times we are in.
I admire anyone who leads well, especially through the thick and thin.

Back to strong foundations. Everyone in this country must chip in.
The family unit—the pillar of society—build yours strong within.
No matter how your family is, never give up.
Remember it *takes two to tango*, and you can still have a win.

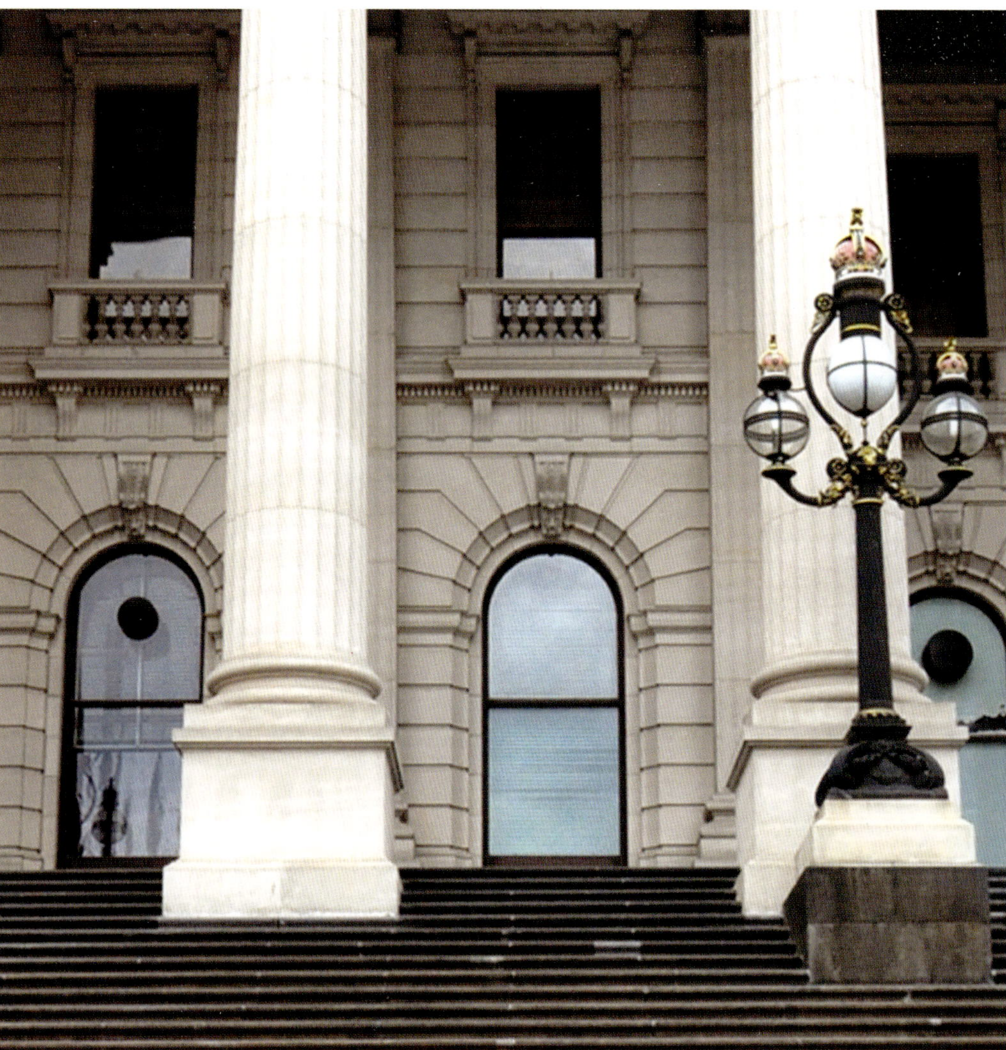

Parliament House *continued...*

Get back to being a giver, like our nations' pioneers in the start
What birthed Parliament's daily ritualism: *Your kingdom come, your will be done*
Our leaders rising up as our heroes, maintaining this
Attitude of heart.

Painting *Parliament House* [Previous page]
I felt the tram really helps complete this picture, giving it a 'just-right' feel for the subject. I deliberately chose to have people of different races walking up the stairs to portray our multi-cultural city. The purpose of the red-purple tinge of sky was to create a daring vibration of colour against the greys of the building, in an effort to lift the picture out of the ordinary.

Photo *A segment of Victorian Parliament House* [Left]
Men and women of our Parliament House are the crucial pillars of our society for the leadership they provide. You can see these pillars are beautifully sculpted, especially as you stand up close. I would have liked to have taken more shots of the pillars themselves, especially using the afternoon light to create exciting shades, but on that day almost the entire facade was under renovation!
The lesson is, we need to be flexible. I only had a tiny little section without scaffolding so I made the most of it.

Tip Don't be quick to withdraw from seemingly difficult obstructed views. Allow the 'difficult' to become a catalyst for the creative mind.

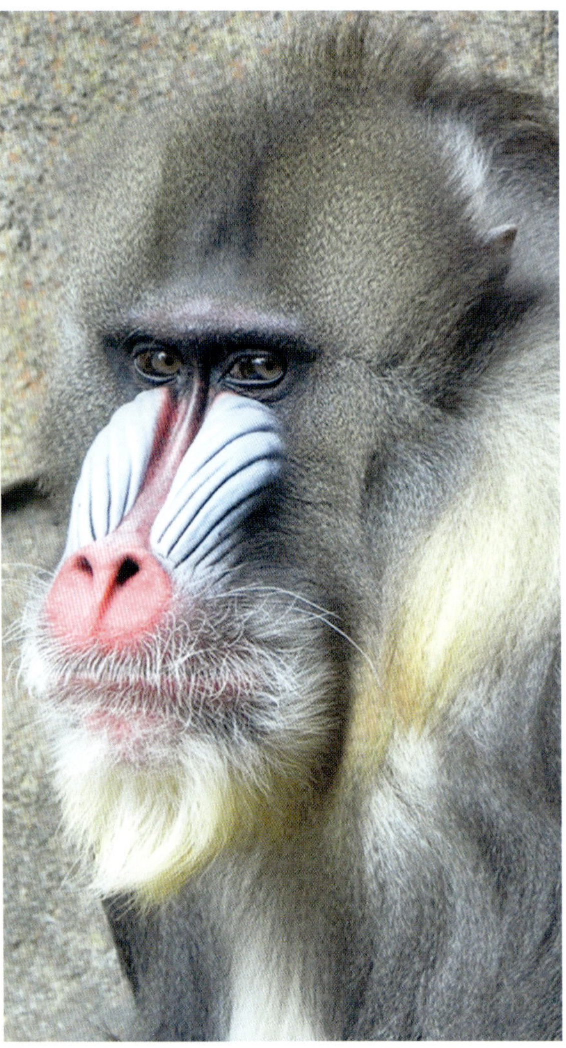

Photo

Mandrill, The Melbourne Zoo [Left] The Mandrill appears to be looking right at home as he looks intently into the camera as if posing for his portrait.

The Melbourne Zoo

The Zoo. Haven for the world's animals from every place
Tackling the threat of extinction head on, it's the planet they face.

The Zoo. A magnet for the crowds, families and kids not a few
Beautiful moments together; come and view—

Elephant trunk so long and thin
Like a vacuum, he takes the food in.

Kangaroo hops up and down
Like perfect car suspension, he bounces all around.

Sleepy koala eating delicate gum leaves
Like a gentle little juice extractor, he gets what he needs.

Superb green parrot, most gorgeous green you will see
Like a soldier in camouflage, hidden in front of you on a tree.

Orang-utan so clever, he glides from here to there
His arms are like elastic bands. What he does no one would dare.

Mandrills are such characters. With faces like actors, a portrait in a cast.
Is it a case of too much make up, or is he truly wearing a mask?

Emus are such a tall bird, towering above mankind
His legs appear like a camera stand, lanky when each section unwinds.

The Zoo. Despite all the incredible animals, the wackiest-best is still
man by far. Why is he so different? Why is he *the star?*

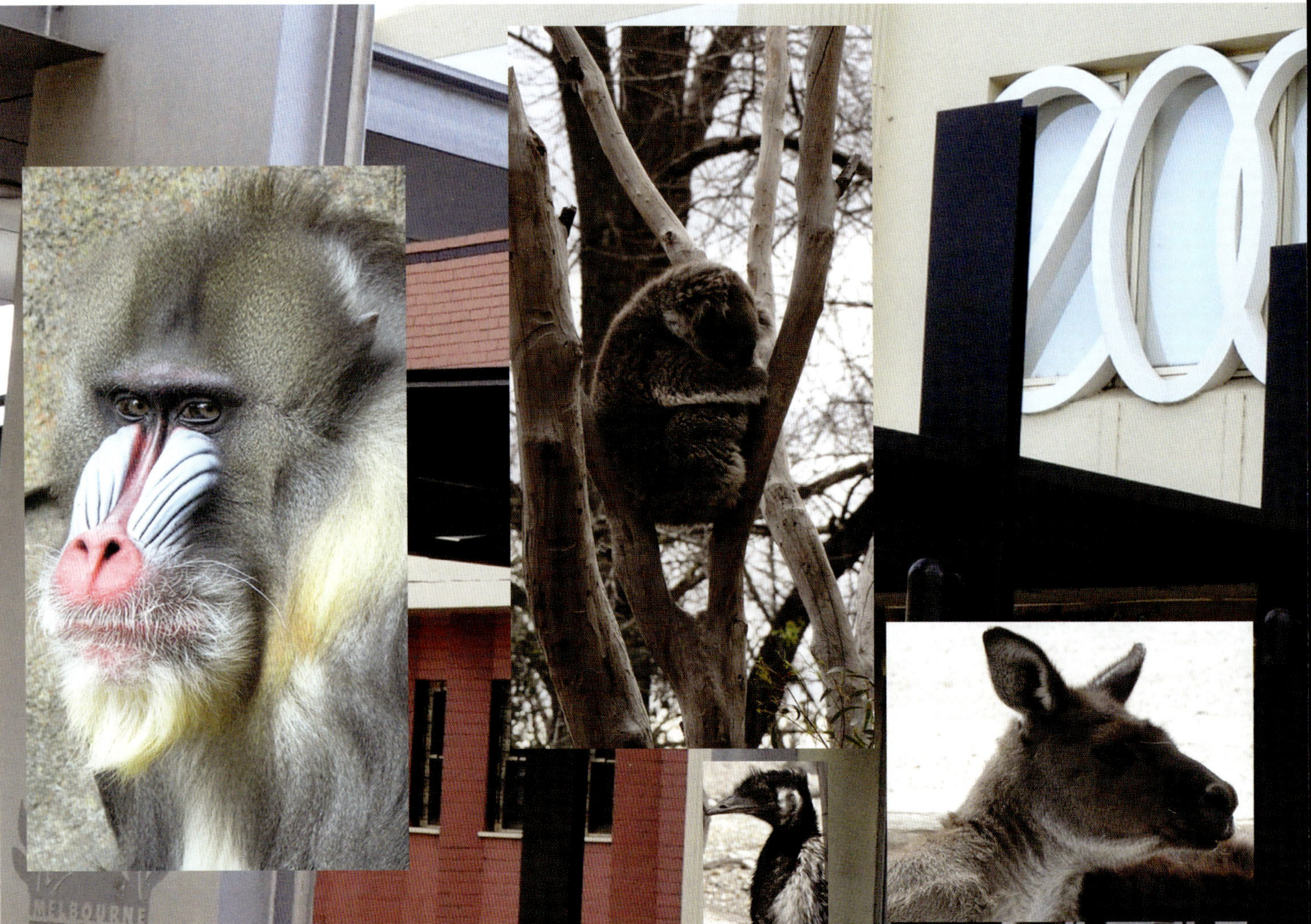
MELBOURNE

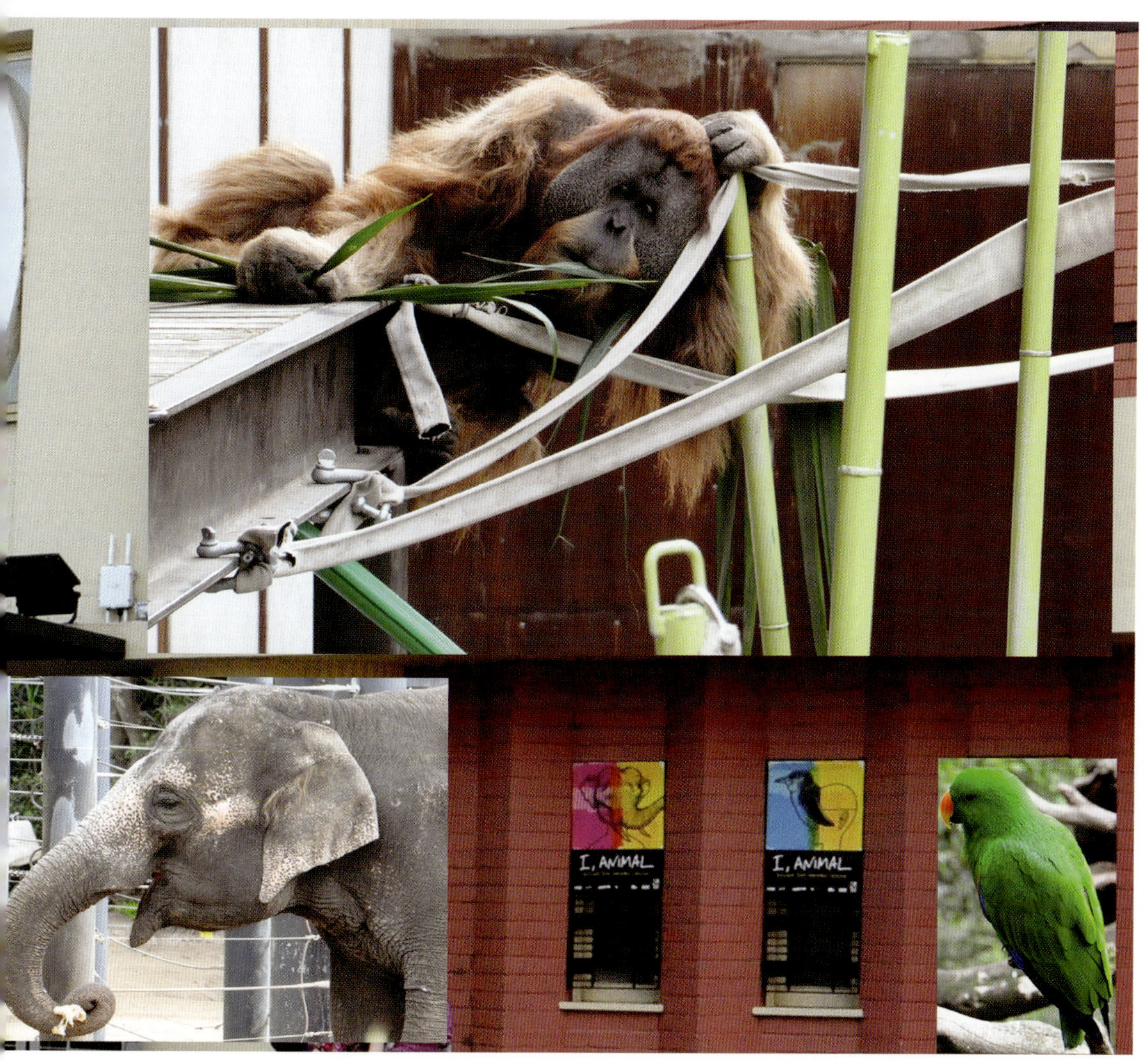

Photo *The Melbourne Zoo, various exhibits* [Left]
It was a joy to walk about the Royal Melbourne Zoo. Here are some of my favourite animals. I watched intently as the Orang-utan began merrily gliding about his space. This shot really epitomises his antics!

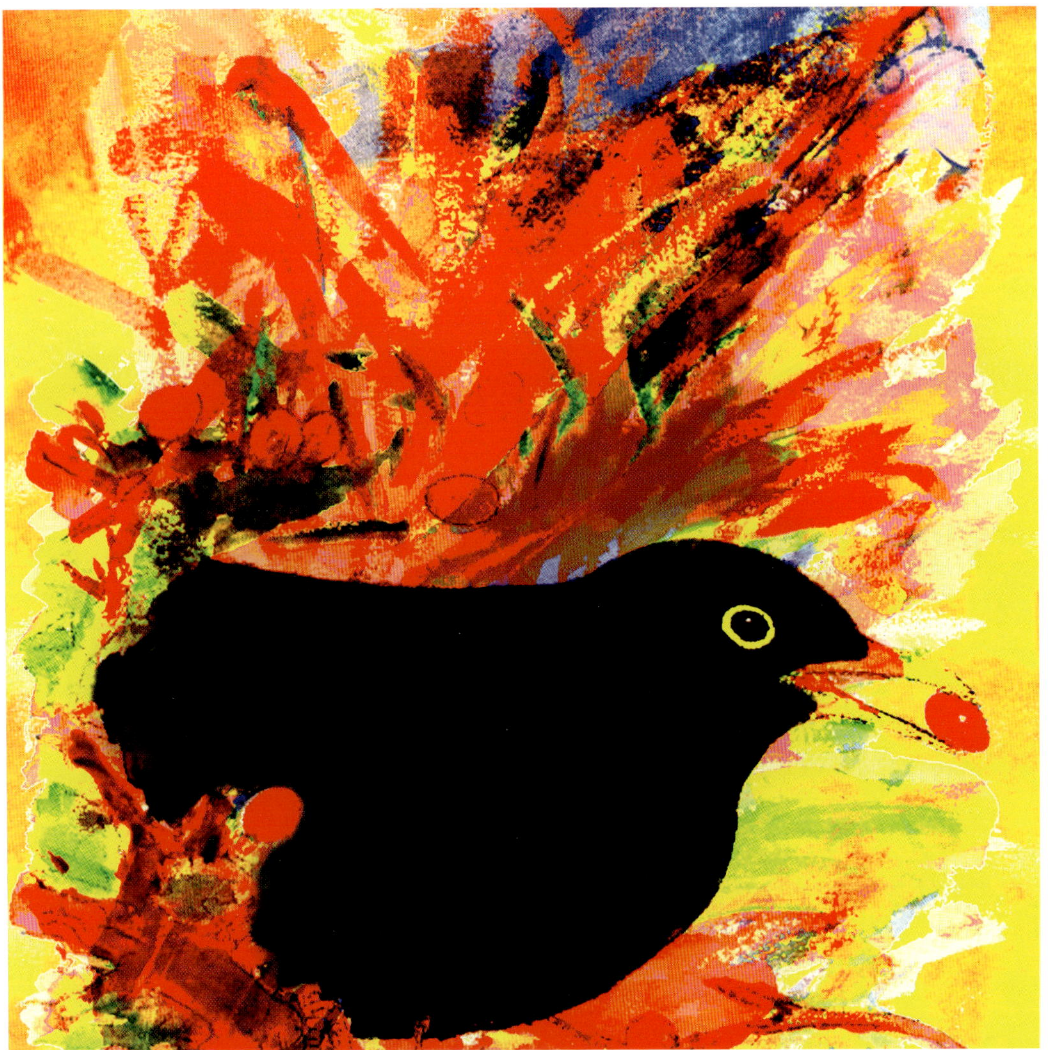

Painting *Blackbird* [Left]

The sparrows and blackbirds constantly provided wonderful company for my seventeen month-old daughter and I during the photo tour. Despite all the majestic zoo animals, she often seemed more impressed by these birds as they came up close. The blackbird is very special to me. This is one of my first paintings.

Tip Keep painting and designing even during those times when people don't seem to value your work. (Example: Interestingly, just prior to doing this Blackbird painting my wife commented on some of my earlier attempts to paint, she said that even my little niece, who is seven years old, could draw better!)

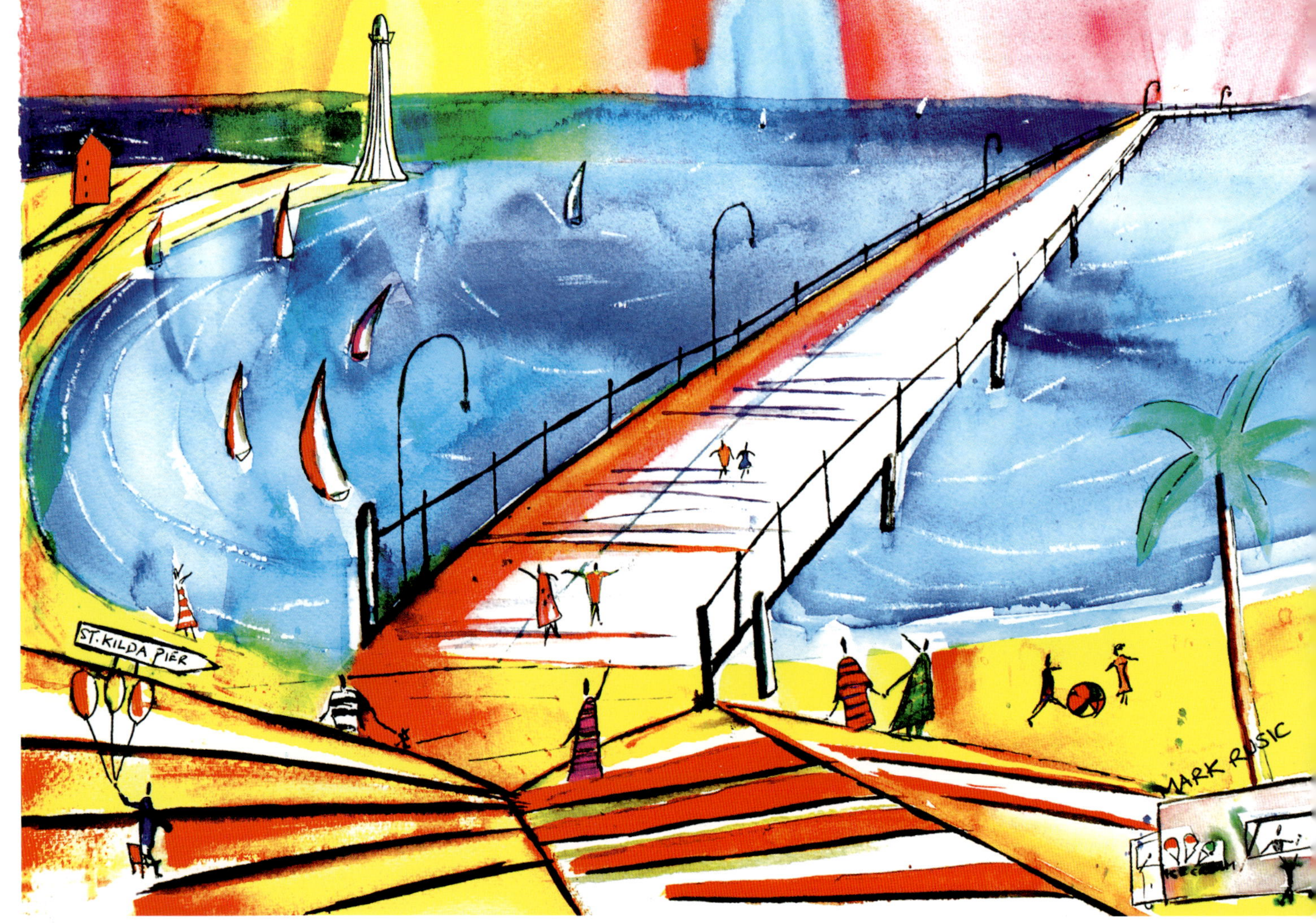
ST. KILDA PIER
MARK RUSIC

Painting *St Kilda Beach* [Left]
A customer who bought this piece and had lived in the area for years told me, 'You have perfectly captured the vibe of St Kilda.' It's words like these that help you know you are making a difference in people's lives!

Photo *St Kilda Beach* [Right]
Note: I used this very view of St Kilda Beach to conjure up my artwork. Many things in the scene inspired me. But, I invite you to compare the artwork with the photo to see what I actually painted. I say 'Art is imagination on canvas'. It is also about making crucial choices about what to focus on.

Tip Be selective in what you paint. Avoid cluttering the scene with too many objects or things. Note: I did not paint everything I saw. When painting, ask yourself: What are you trying to achieve? What is the chief end or motif of the painting? Focus on that and bring it out well!

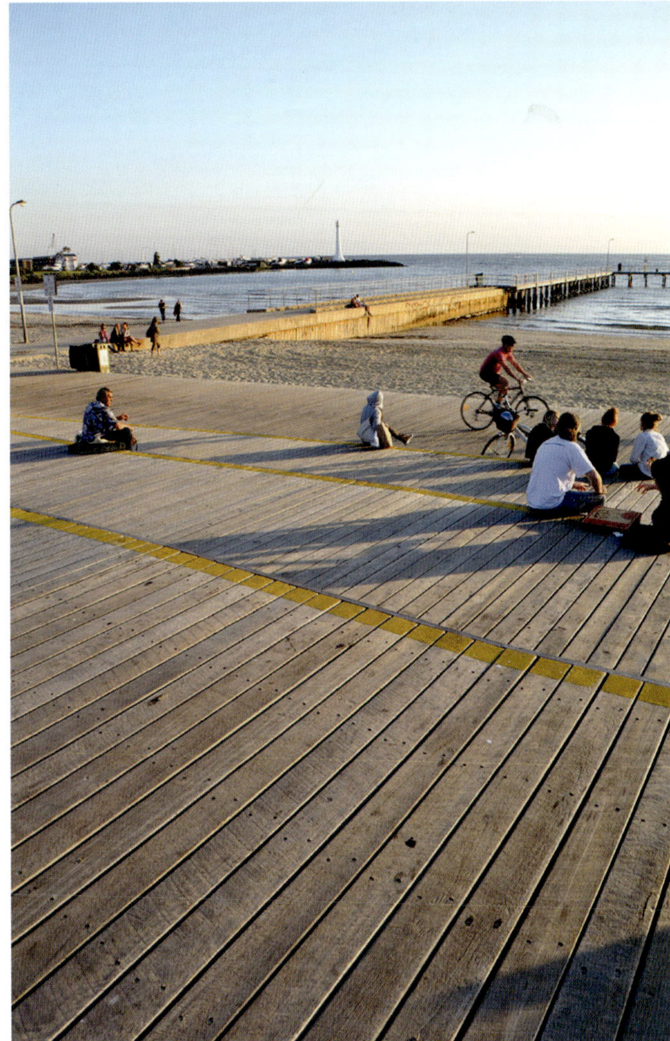

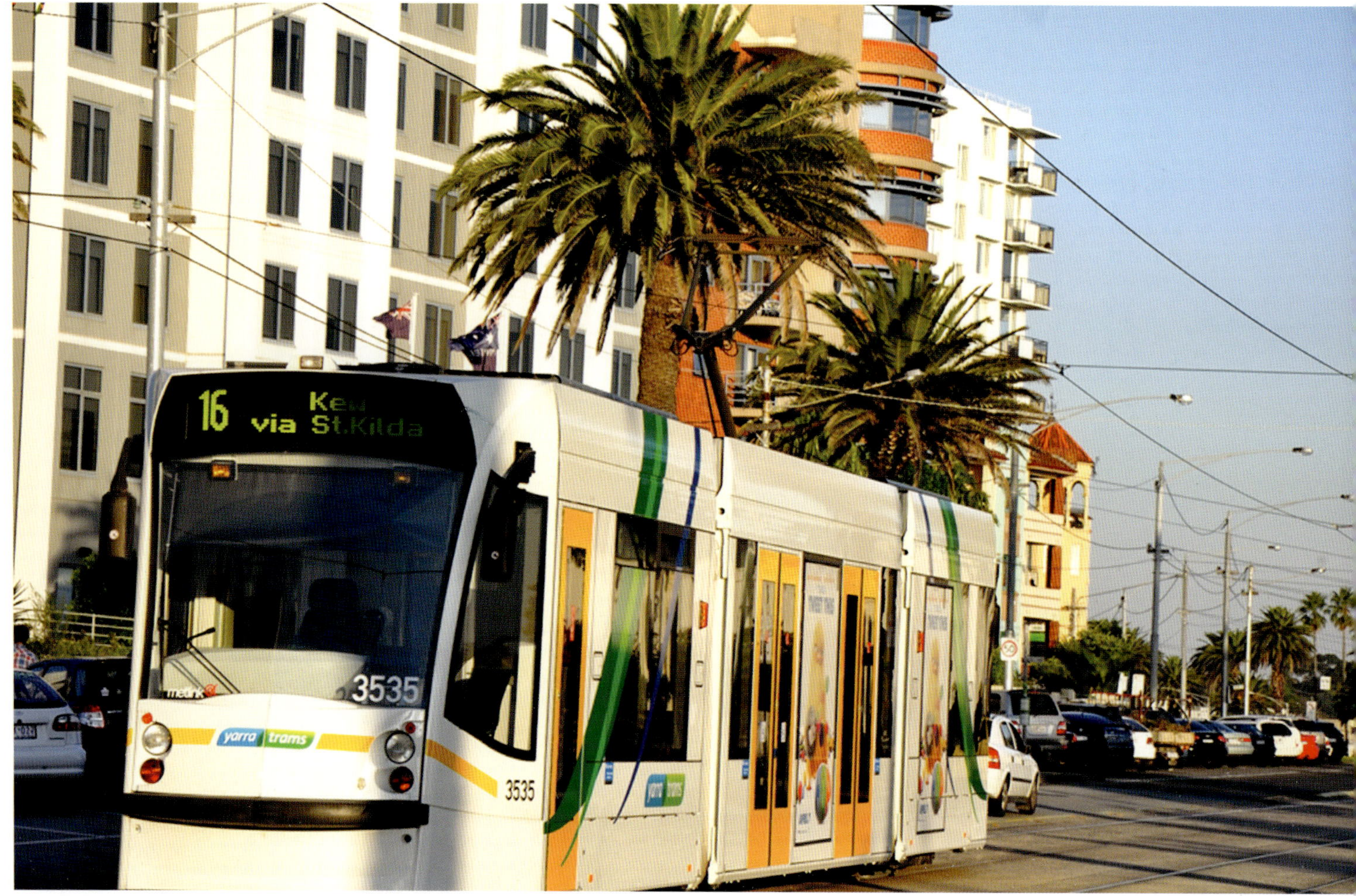

Photo The trams play a special part in creating *the vibe and excitement in Beautiful St Kilda*. [Above]

St Kilda Beach

Beautiful St Kilda - blue and golden jewel
Beautiful St Kilda - magnetic attraction whether the weather is warm or cool

Beautiful St Kilda - wind surfing, sunbathing and the life outdoors
Beautiful St Kilda - the vibe, excitement, the trams and so much more

Beautiful girl - on daddy's knee
Beautiful girl - loved, adored, secure in her destiny

Beautiful girl - walking with her daddy by the sea
Beautiful girl - eyes on that light house, clear direction for you and me

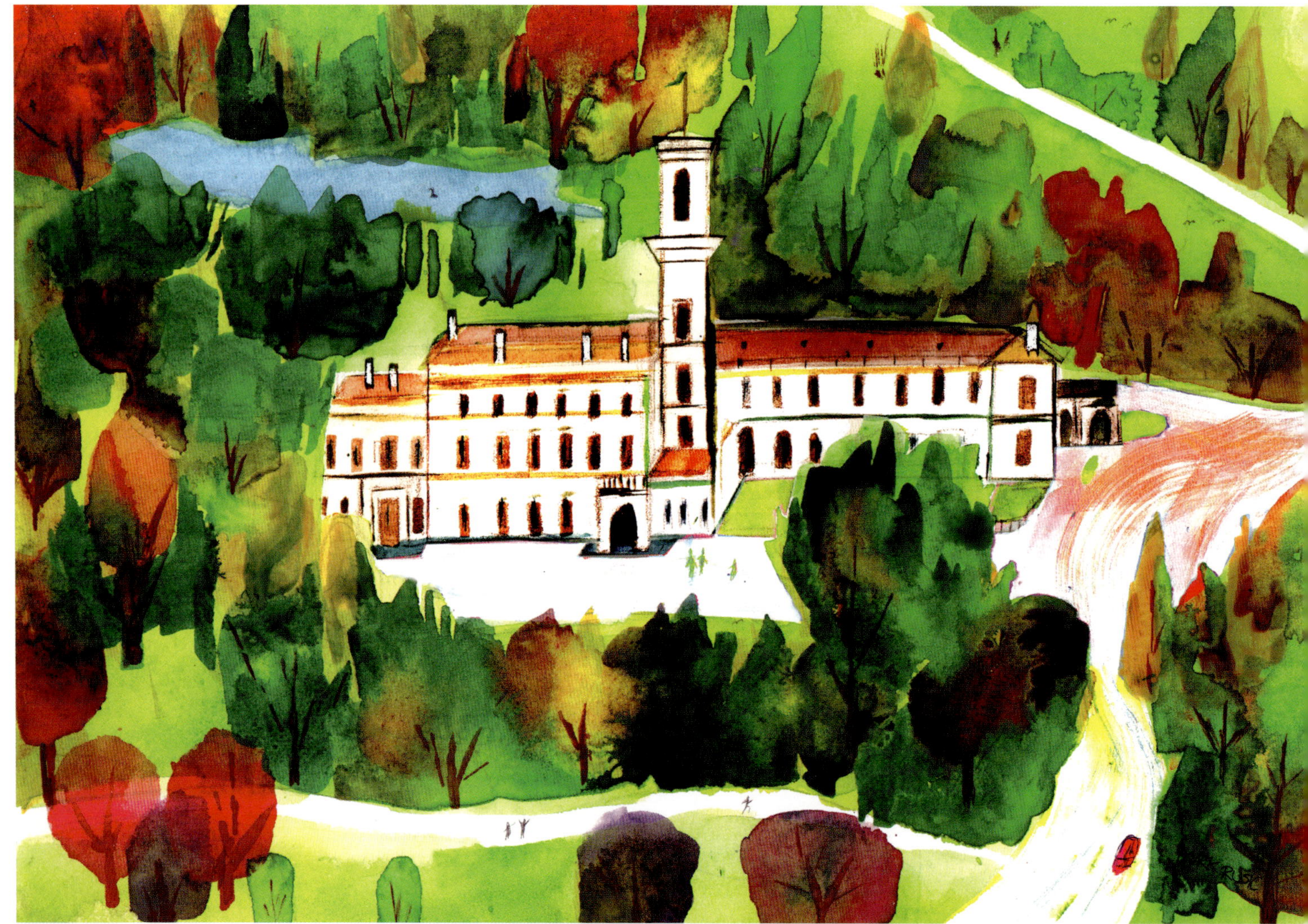

Royal Botanic Gardens Melbourne

Oh the beauty of nature. Therapy for the soul and mind.
A peaceful paradise adjacent to the busy CBD—
Royal Botanic Gardens
you'll find. Despite the ravaging influences of
climate and the world's strife
Pristine Gardens preserved for us all—one of a kind

Strolling through the city
Are gardens 'for me' with my busy pace of life?
Bliss as I enter the RBG gates. Leafy green pathways
Peace cuts out the noise of the city, clean like a knife.
Now I can ponder the big picture—
What am I'm really doing with my time?
The Garden's call…
green lawns, lie down on that cushion of grass, unwind!

Indeed, the Gardens are a gift to the City. To be enjoyed primarily.
Amazing selection of plants. Mind-boggling numbers of species.
Sheer pleasure to see.
It begun with planted seeds in 1846. A garden millennium's ago.
Imagine how many generations have walked these grounds for us?

So,

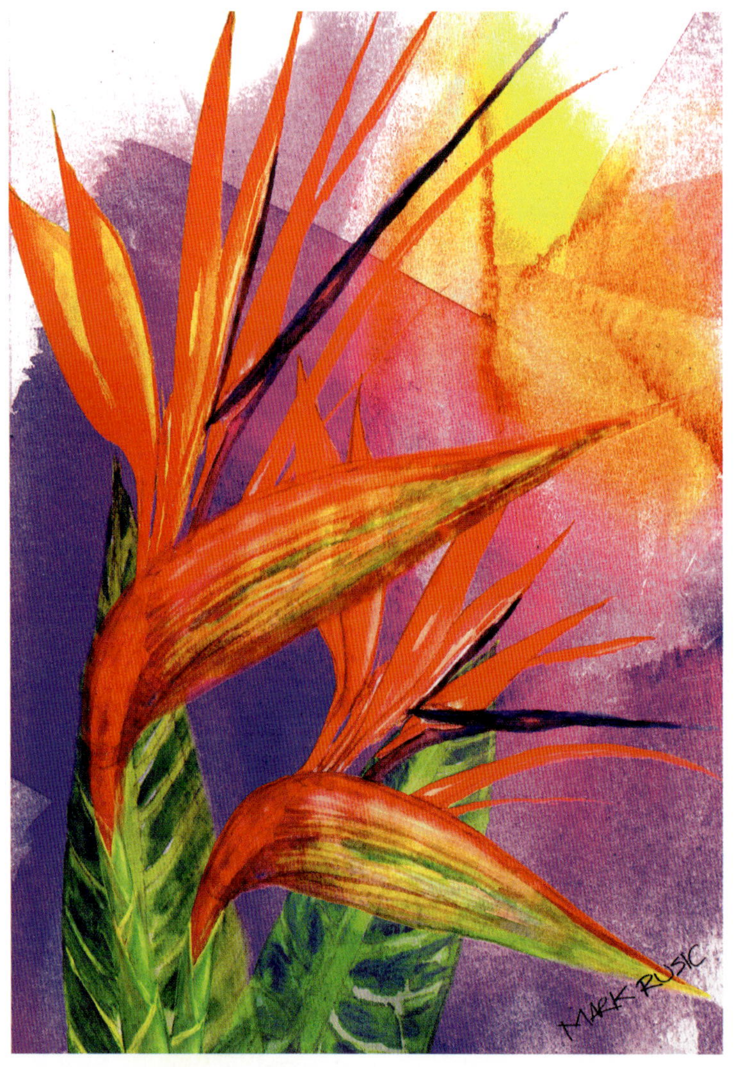

Painting	*Bird of Paradise* [Left] One of my favourite flowers is the Bird of Paradise; there are many at the Gardens.
Tip	One of the main motivations in painting is to take pleasure in what you paint. You paint better that way.

Royal Botanic Gardens Melbourne *continued...*

let's take care of our planet. Less Co2 some people say.
Initiatives to take, we hope, to lead us all to a better day.
Will I use the air-con less? Install solar today?
The audacious task at hand: Make global-warming global-cooled
Big humanity, big planet: For sure more bills to pay!

Care for the environment. Care for the earth.
Go green. Introduce a vegie-patch in your garden;
that neglected turf.
Pick up papers and rubbish without being told
Little eco-friendly efforts for the City
worth their weight in gold.

And, how about caring for the inner garden of mind.
In reducing friction and conflict
Environmental-friendly and people-friendly
we can all unwind.

Painting *Governor House in the Royal Botanic Gardens* [Previous page]
My joy in this painting is the wonderful, contrasting colours of the many trees at autumn time, with dominant greens overall. The simplicity of the Governor's House as central, is iconic.

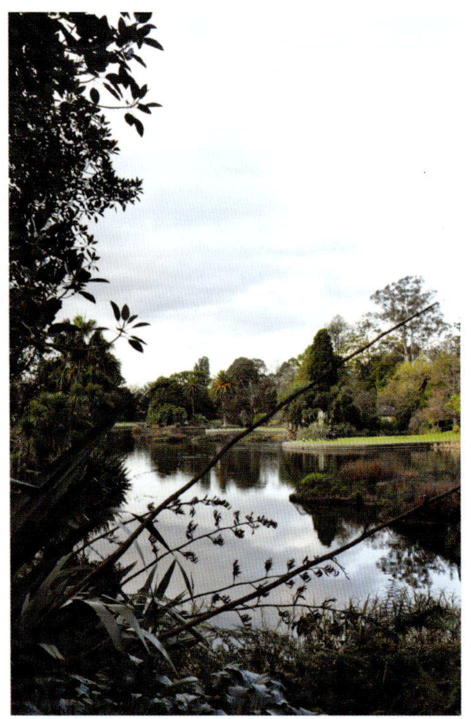

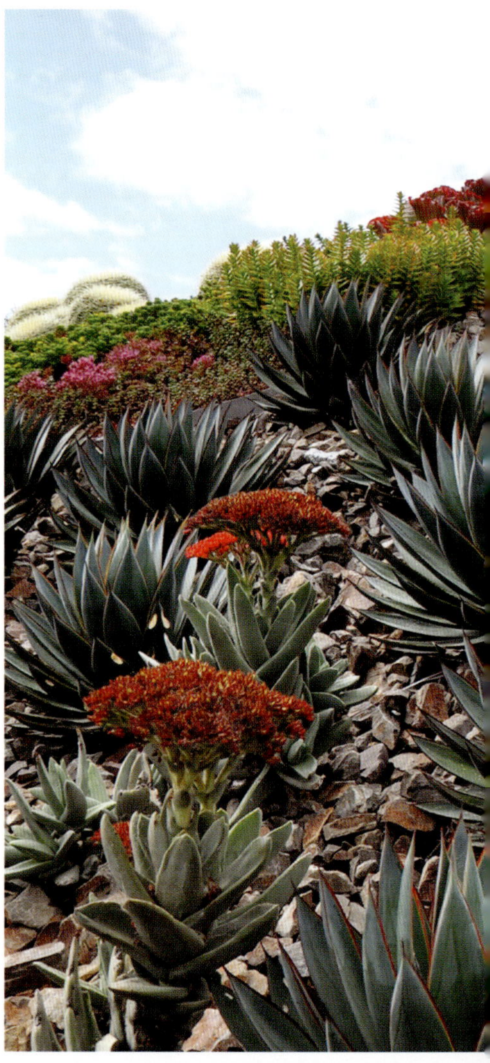

Photo *Lake views, Royal Botanic Gardens* [Above]
What a great peace-haven, recreational paradise we have adjacent to our busy CBD. A great lunch time get away.

Photo *From Guilfoyles Volcano, Royal Botanic Gardens* [Right]
Indeed, an 'amazing selections of plants' are to be found. These lovely Golden Barrel Cacti at the Volcano are among some of my favourites.

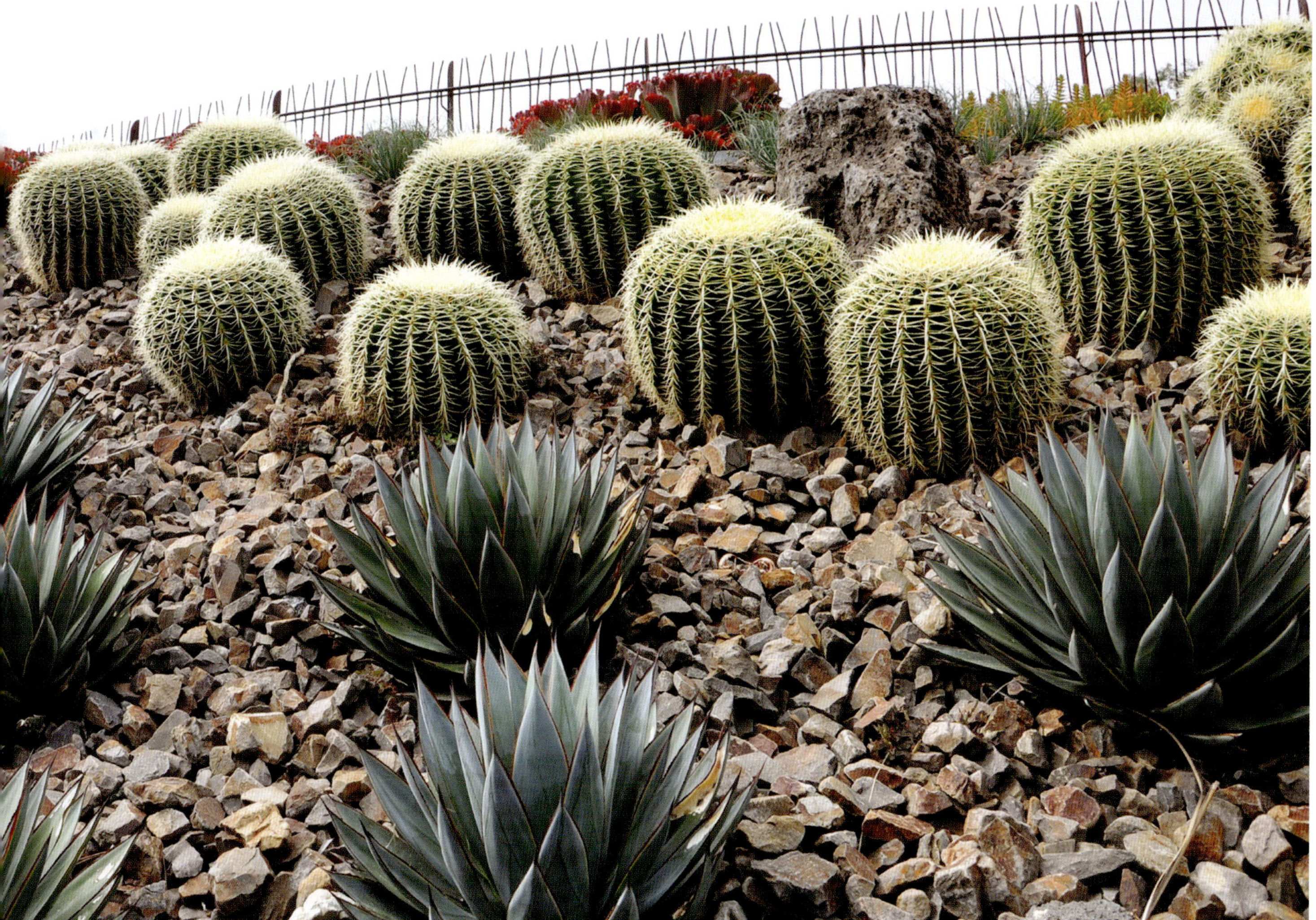

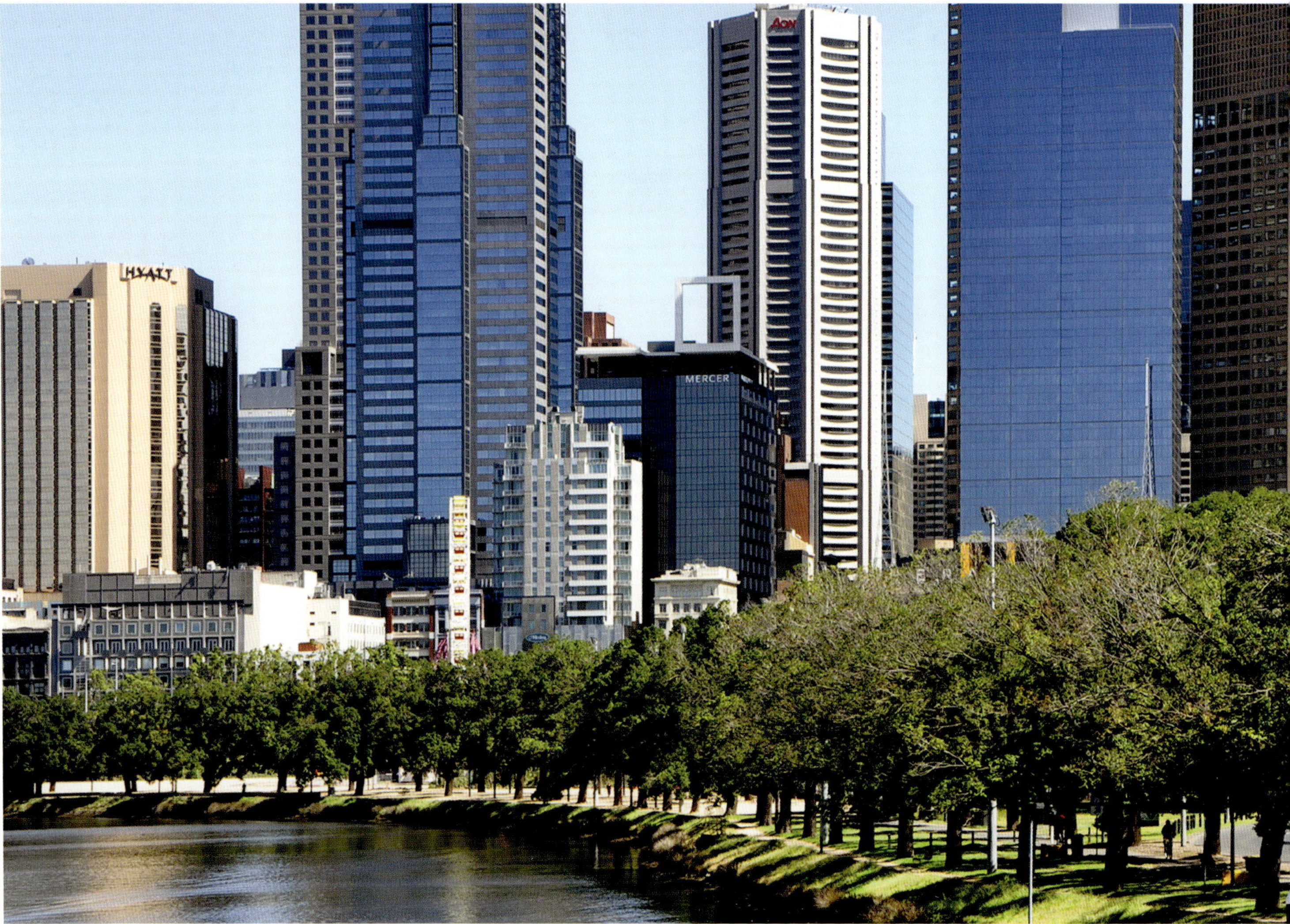
HYATT
AON
MERCER

Iconic Melbourne

…A city with stunning beauty
Reputed *most liveable* in the world
This poem, a reminder of why she's iconic
What those things are about her, for want of a better expression—
that makes straight hair curl?

The retro finishes of Jeff's Shed. Fed.Square. Eureka
New compared to
Old. We've come a long way Melbourne…
She's very very bold!

Dotted about the city. Brightly coloured
trams pass you by from left and right, chugging along. Catch
the green limousine and see her slopes, straights and valleys,
makes the heart burst into song.

Lovely little laneways: Flinders Lane, Degraves Street, The Walk Arcade...
Melbourne is about dining out. Traders always doing a roaring trade.

What I love most is the people
you see. Melbourne
Could not be Melbourne if it was not for you and me!
Friendly, kind-hearted souls not concerned by rank or creed
May Melbourne continue to prosper like the Yarra River bank's, strongest oak trees.

Photo ***CBD with Yarra River*** [Left]
May our city prosper just like these beautiful trees by the Yarra river.

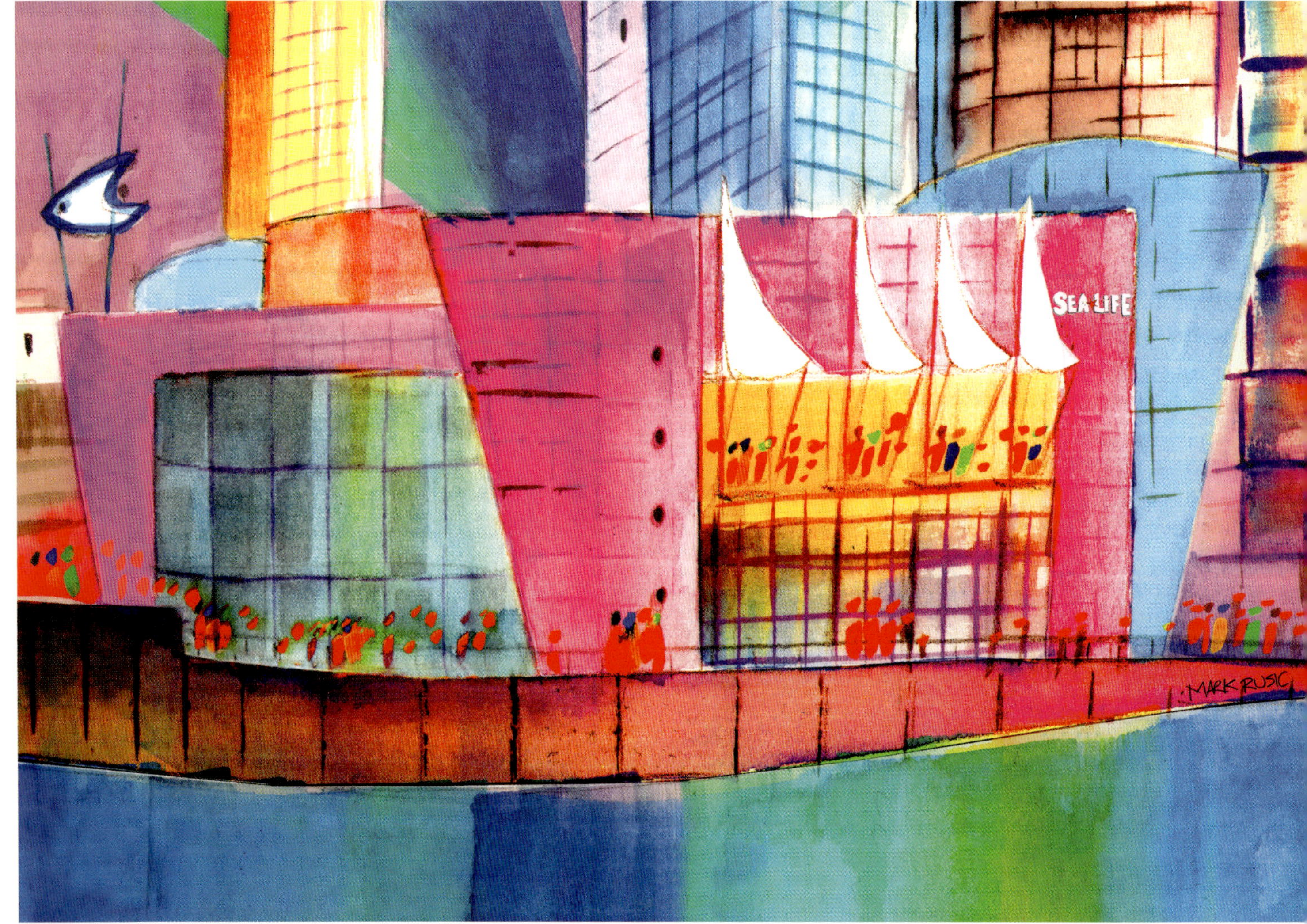
SEA LIFE
MARK RUSIC

SEA LIFE Melbourne Aquarium

The Aquarium of Melbourne. No ordinary place at all.
You can walk under water! Watch incredible SEA LIFE gargantuan and small.
Did you know a whole new world, under the ocean waters, you find
Strange and wonderful creatures from the depths.
And there's my unusual parallel-like migration, something to tease our minds.

When I see schools of fish racing about together in unison,
appearing to have so much fun, I wonder why prejudice among
different races sometimes exists. Why can't the many nations also be as one?

Like the tortoise, slow and steady
And sometimes quick to act like the shark
We cannot afford not to move and be one, lest we are torn apart.
That's what the aquarium does. It hosts every kind as one.
If we pursue harmony like that school of fish
We can't help but be blessed,
every nation under the sun.

Our nation's past and future is built on immigration,
So don't blow up like the puffer fish
The world, like the ocean, is big enough. Let many more into your heart.
Remember: acceptance and kindness shown to you,
helped you make a good start...

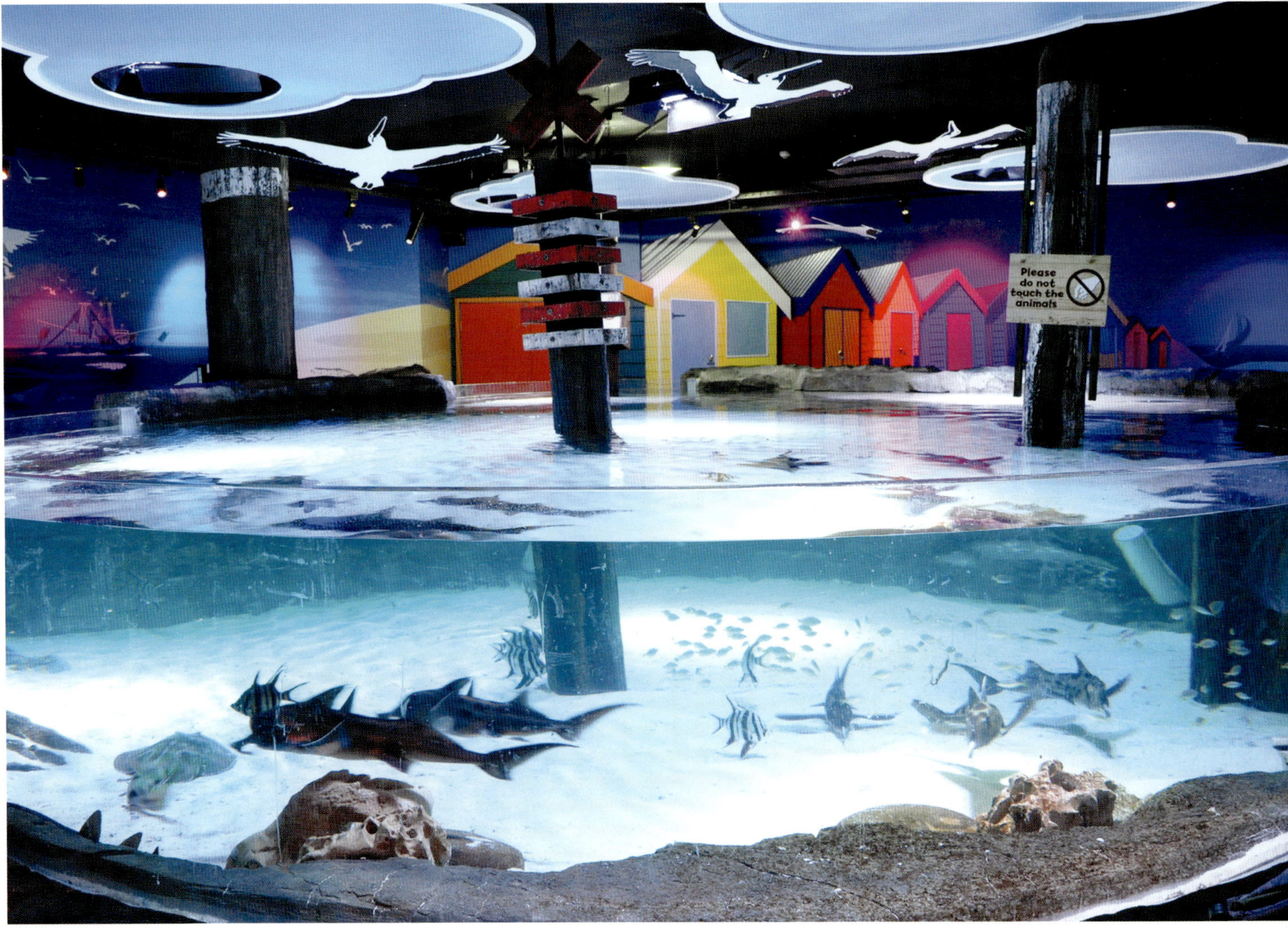
Please
do not
touch the
animals

SEA LIFE Melbourne Aquarium *continued...*

...Dolphin standing, waiting to meet you as he laughs, twists and bends
Now is a time to go out of your way and make new friends.
Thanks to the aquarium, for loving all the fishes, and for 'Mega Croc' and the seals,
for giving us this treasure and access—this experience. It's excellent. And real.

Painting — *SEA LIFE Melbourne Aquarium* [Previous page]
The idea was to bring out the 'jewel' of the aquarium's design through this painting. This is my night view. I have tried to show how funky it is with some of these extreme colours at work. The aquarium is a cool place to go.

Photo — *SEA LIFE Melbourne Aquarium Exhibit* [Left]
The staff work hard to make all the exhibits top quality. This one really caught my eye and also has some schools of fish as mentioned in the poem.

Tip — There is always a tension between a pursuit of one's dream and keeping family life in balance. Some of us go for broke to make our vision come to pass only to discover it was a severe cost to family relationships. Note: Quality and well-nurtured relationships struggle to stay alive in the 'desert of obsession'. This is crucial to understand if you are starting a business or embarking on a personal project, especially 'on the side' while carrying a day-job. What do you do, especially if you have kids, so it all works? A major key is to work at things together as a family. If all can play some part and feel connected, it's a great step forward. I remember visiting the aquarium as a family. Having a purpose to incorporate the aquarium into the book provided an added sense of excitement. We went about at a casual pace and thoroughly enjoyed the displays. I took a few photos. At the same time my wife provided some valuable counsel on what shots might work best. It was also a great opportunity to expose my daughter to this amazing underwater world. Our highlight was simply being together. Doing this book was a bonus.

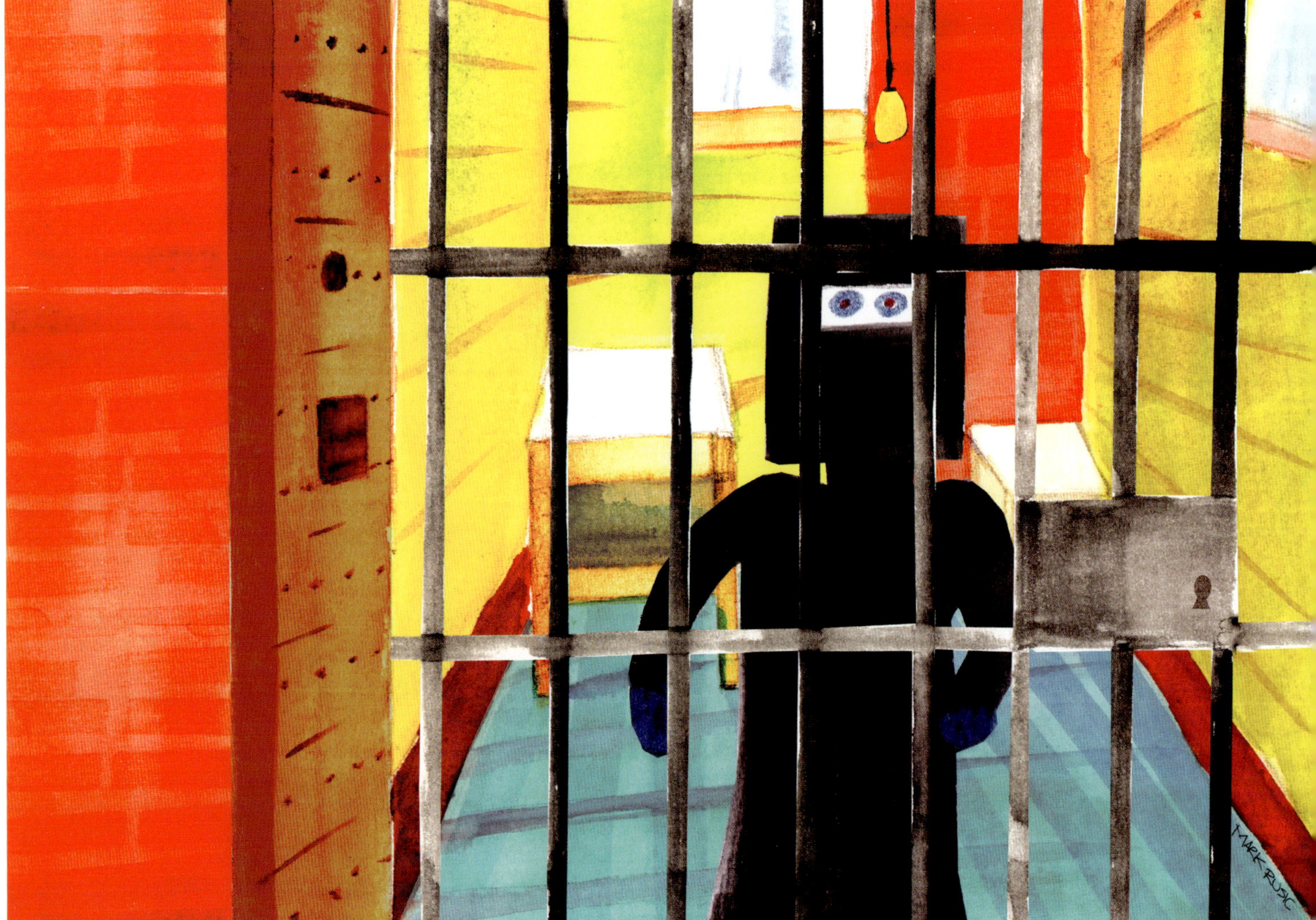
MARK RUSIC

Old Melbourne Gaol

Prisoners in the depths of darkness, paying dues, brought down low.
Hung from cold concrete gallows, for stolen bread or stolen life, a life of woes.
Ned Kelly from Glenrowan, criminal-bushranger, our most infamous hero.
Old Melbourne Gaol. No comforts like prison today. No
TV, no easy paroles, no conjugal rights. No go.

No easy task the administration of justice.
Hardened criminals continue to rebel, take the law into their own hands.
Does a life behind bars even make amends...

This world needs justice. The challenge is to apply justice with compassion
and love. We all fall short of God's glory. No one's perfect like the One above.
Justice. Stinging punishment given, a clear deterrent, producing fear.
And yet with every effort to restore dignity, with faith in people
Just imagine the person doing time could be you or those you hold dear.

Best not to even test the justice system in the first place.
Just imagine those prison window bars…

No joy in doing time, so careful what you do.
When they say easy money, think twice, before joining the wrong crew.
People flow with the tide. But. You have a choice.
Many a life cut short in its prime, so listen out for The Voice.

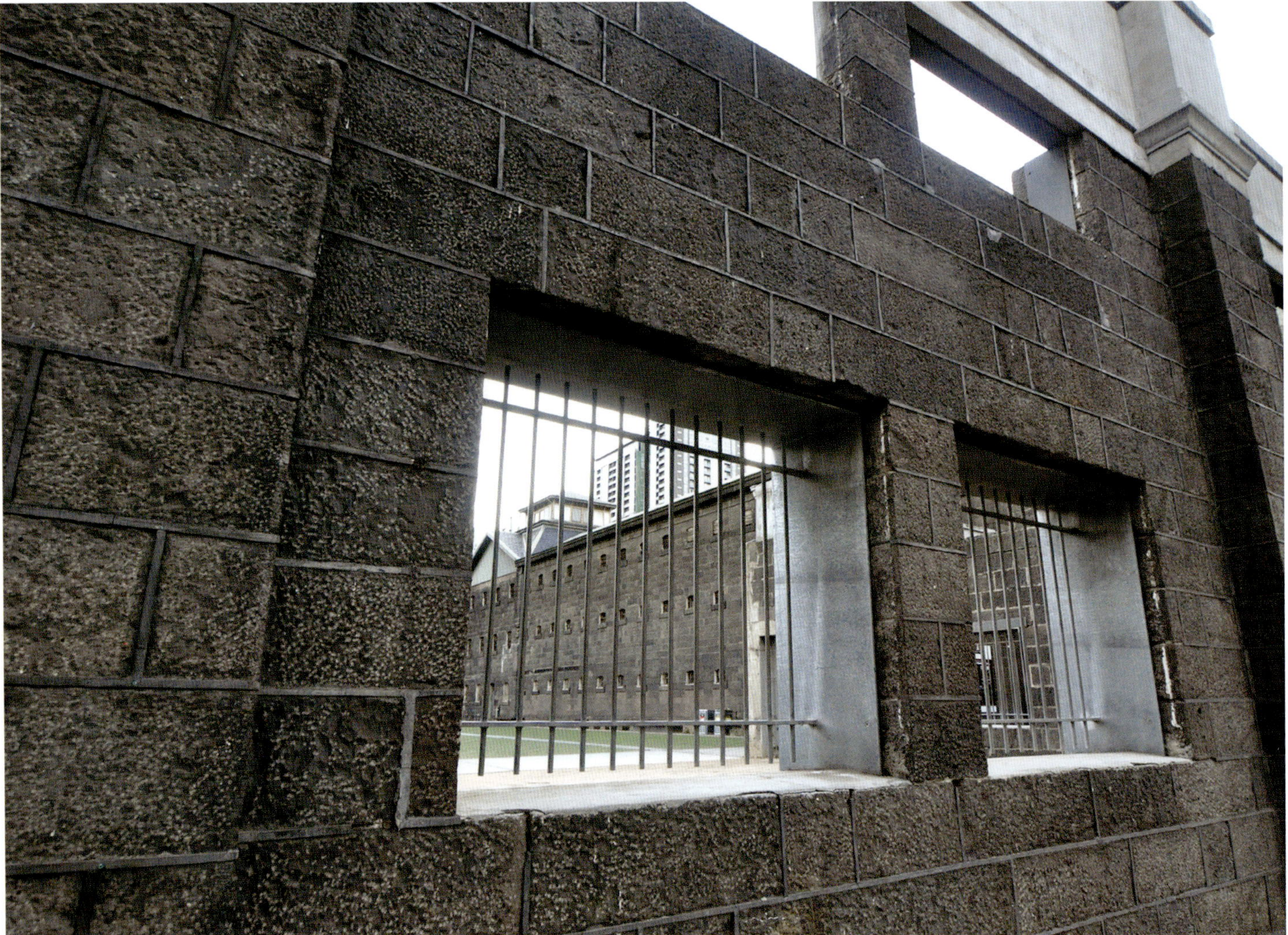

Old Melbourne Gaol *continued...*

Regardless of where you are today, regardless of your past
turn it all around this week, and live a life to last.
Light is here. Light is there. No need to be in the dark.
The only question for you and I is, How
will your life make an endearing mark?

Painting	*I was imagining Ned Kelly when arrested and put in a cell* [Previous page] So, my picture is fictitious. But, the idea was to use some creative license and take the mundane and attempt to transform it into the something vibrant and captivating.
Tip	Using artistic license means that the most dull and ordinary setting or subject has great potential.
Photo	*The Old Melbourne Gaol is a National Trust of Australia (Victoria) property.* [Left] The photo is simple and seeks to highlight the 'drag feeling' of what it means to be behind bars, especially in those times. Hence, the poem says, 'just imagine those prison window bars...'

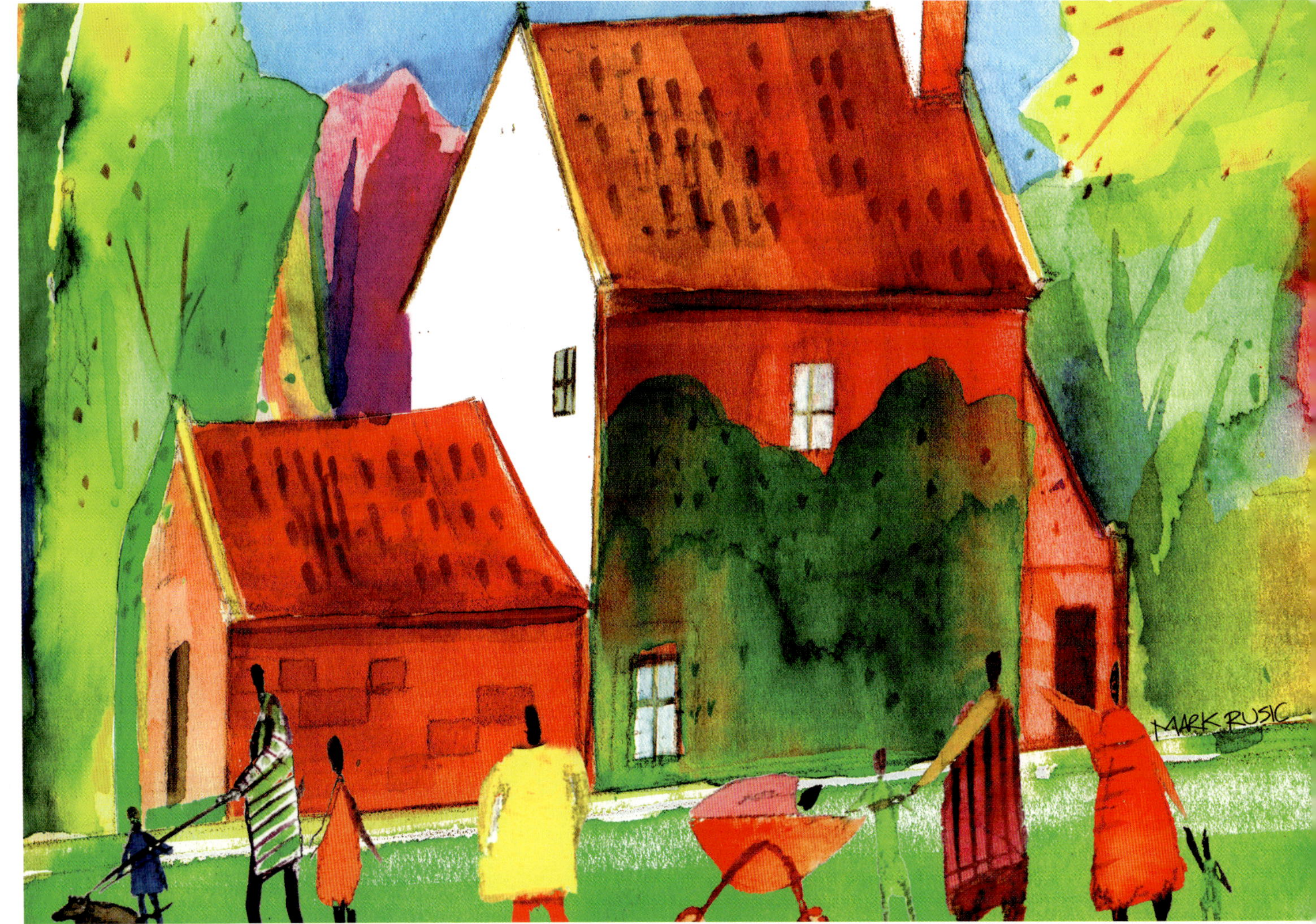
MARK RUSIC

Cooks' Cottage

Nestled in the Gardens. You stumble upon a wonderful little home.
A reminder of a simpler place from where, a man would roam
Captain Cook. Bold adventurer. Innovator.
He went where no man had gone before.
A great price he paid. As have so many others so that we, today, might have more.

Time to acknowledge the ones who made way for us all
Who made for us platforms upon which, we might all stand tall
Made of them: parents, teachers, business men, carers, leaders—
Now we have a future. We cannot give up or be tempted to stall.

Now it is our turn to rise. Go where others before us could not.
Use the resources and opportunities afforded by the times and
our great city. Don't allow yourself to be spoiled or rot.
Look to the many of great learning; the terabits of information at hand
The countless books, but no substitute for the passion,
determination and endurance, in all our 'Captain Cooks'.

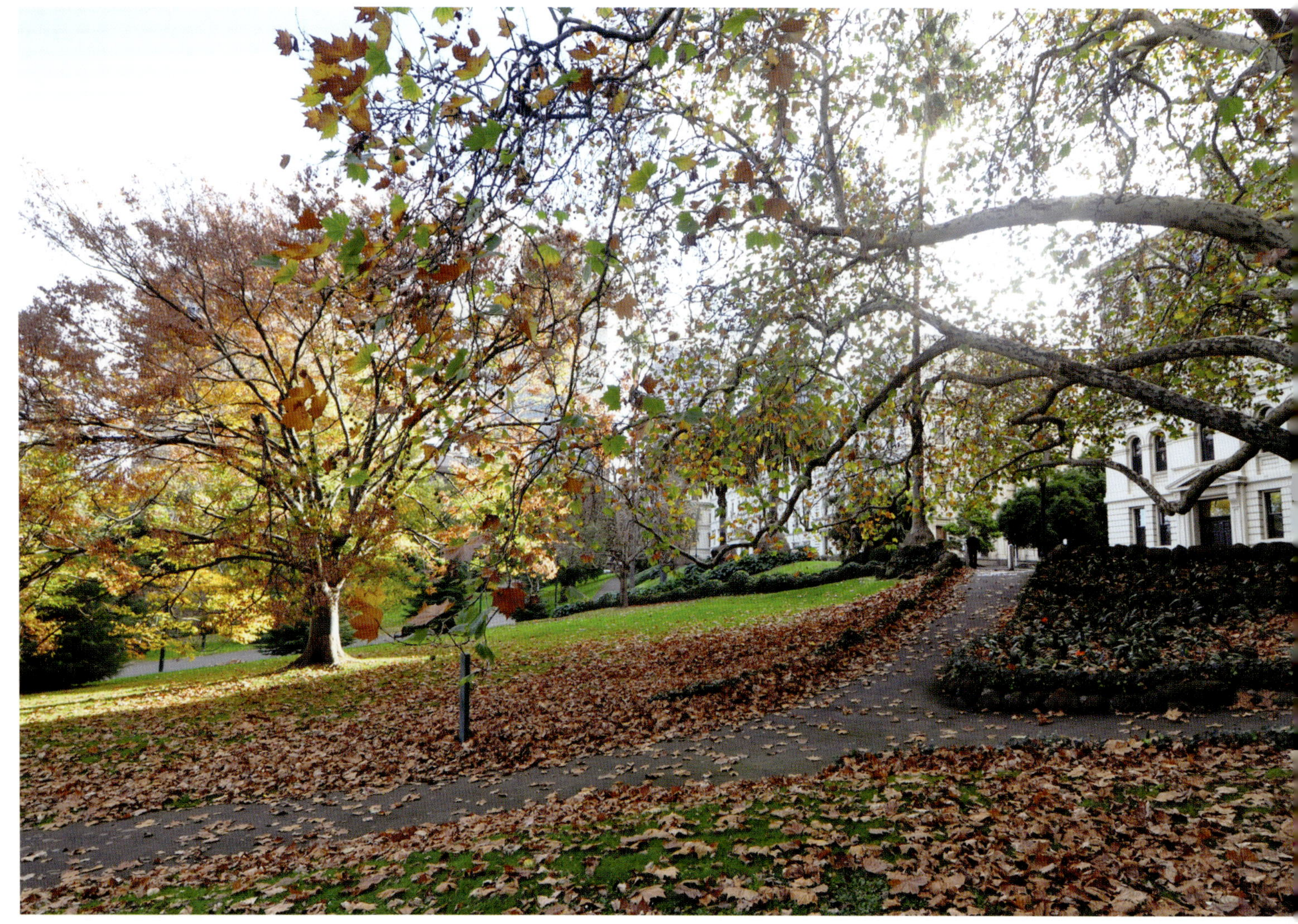

Painting *Cooks' Cottage, Fitzroy Gardens* [Previous page]
What I like about the surrounding gardens is the layered branches and contrasting colours. That glazing effect is one of the great glories of watercolour painting.

Tip To become more innovative: What am I working on today in view of my long-term goal? Consider: what I see tomorrow is the product of my innovative thought of today. Dump the mindset of making a quick dollar, instead focus on producing quality and taking pride in what you do. Business will come naturally. Focus on serving people and their needs and not being served. Never buy into cynicism; creativity best flows out of optimism. Come to terms with your area of passion and pain. Pain relates to feeling frustrated by things you desire to see distinctly improved. It could be anything at all. For example, it pains you that ice cream melts so quickly! You see it dribbling down your child's face so fast and are irritated. Or perhaps you feel there are not enough kid's books about good manners. Or maybe as an entertainer, you feel aren't more song lyrics with a 'happily married' theme? The point is you see and feel the weight of those issues; you can make a difference! So, as you understand your passion and pain you will be best positioned to make a positive contribution and impact on society. And may God bless you.

Photo *Treasury Gardens in front of the Treasury precinct.* [Left]
Cooks' Cottage is located adjacent the Treasury Gardens, 'nestled' in the similarly beautiful Fitzroy Gardens. It was pure pleasure to stand in the midst of this leafy pathway. Melbourne's autumn time is stunning. I am constantly fascinated by its many colours. Melbourne's autumn time is stunning. I am constantly fascinated by its many colours.

Tip Photography is often about an intuitive knowing. Something inside says, 'this scene is it! This is just right.' So shoot fast. To delay a few moments could mean missing the shot completely.

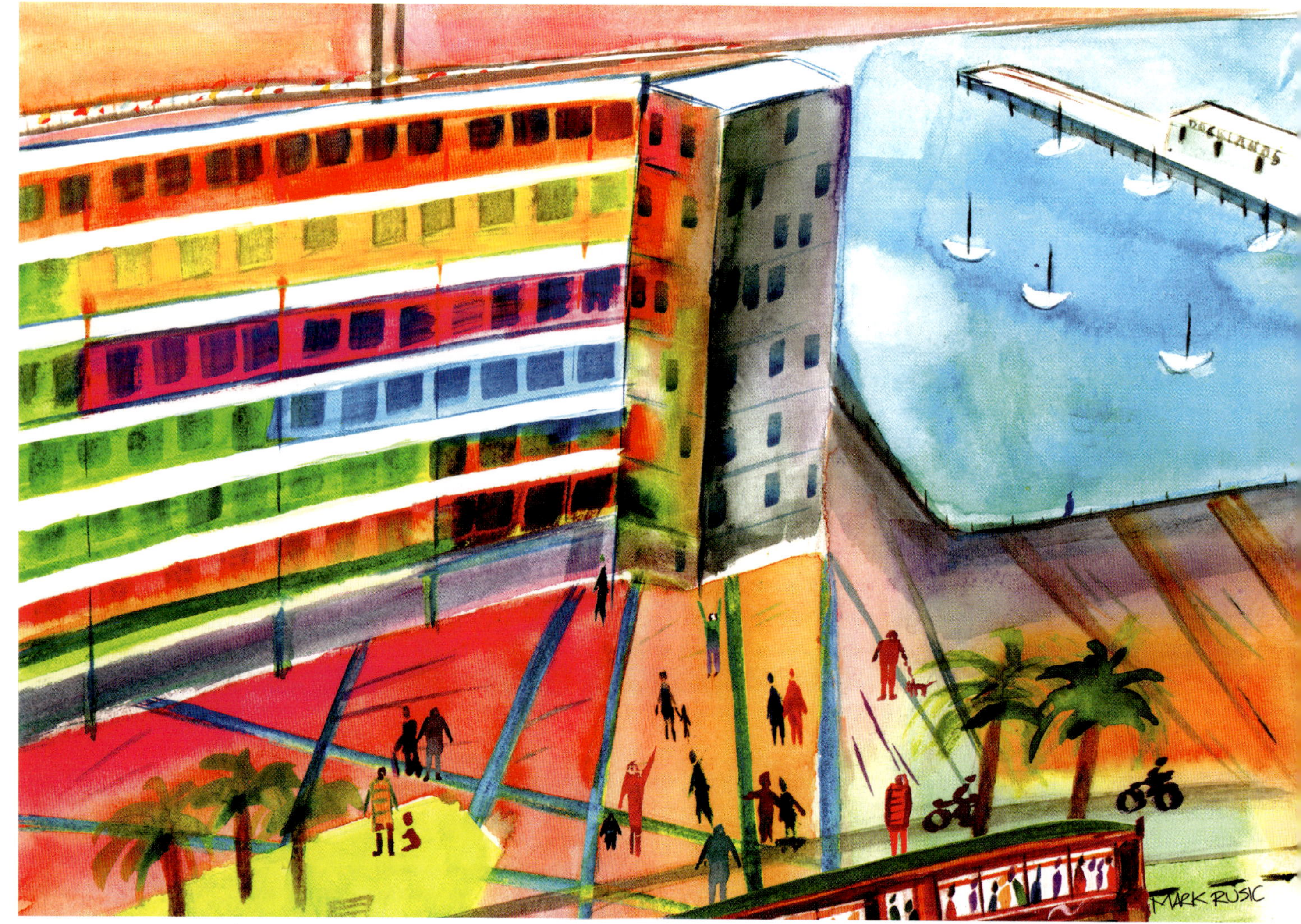
MARK RUSIC

Docklands

Began as a humble swamp a long time ago. Grew into The Docks.
Warfies, painters and dockers, hard men on the edge of crime
In those days, no crowds flocked.
But, today what a marvel when you think how it began.
Now: 'The future of Melbourne City' is
The Docklands

Locals say they love it. Sea views and tram stops all around.
Eye catching buildings, some of the best you'll see in town.
Things to do, restaurants and entertainment alike
It's got 'all that' and more. It's eco-mad. Pathways galore for bikes!

If business has reputation, it's in the Docklands for sure.
The way of doing business has advanced as you will find.
It's all about collaboration. It's all about not wasting time.
Many brains under less roofs, and wireless to the max.
Work as you please. Think outside the square. Minimize the tax.

So, if you say: *I don't live there, what's it all got to do with me?*
Remember, it began as an ugly swamp, an eyesore with some trees.
So, why not do a little home improvement? Those corners you never like to touch?
Open up the kitchen, add a room; do a Dockland mini- appreciation with big bucks!

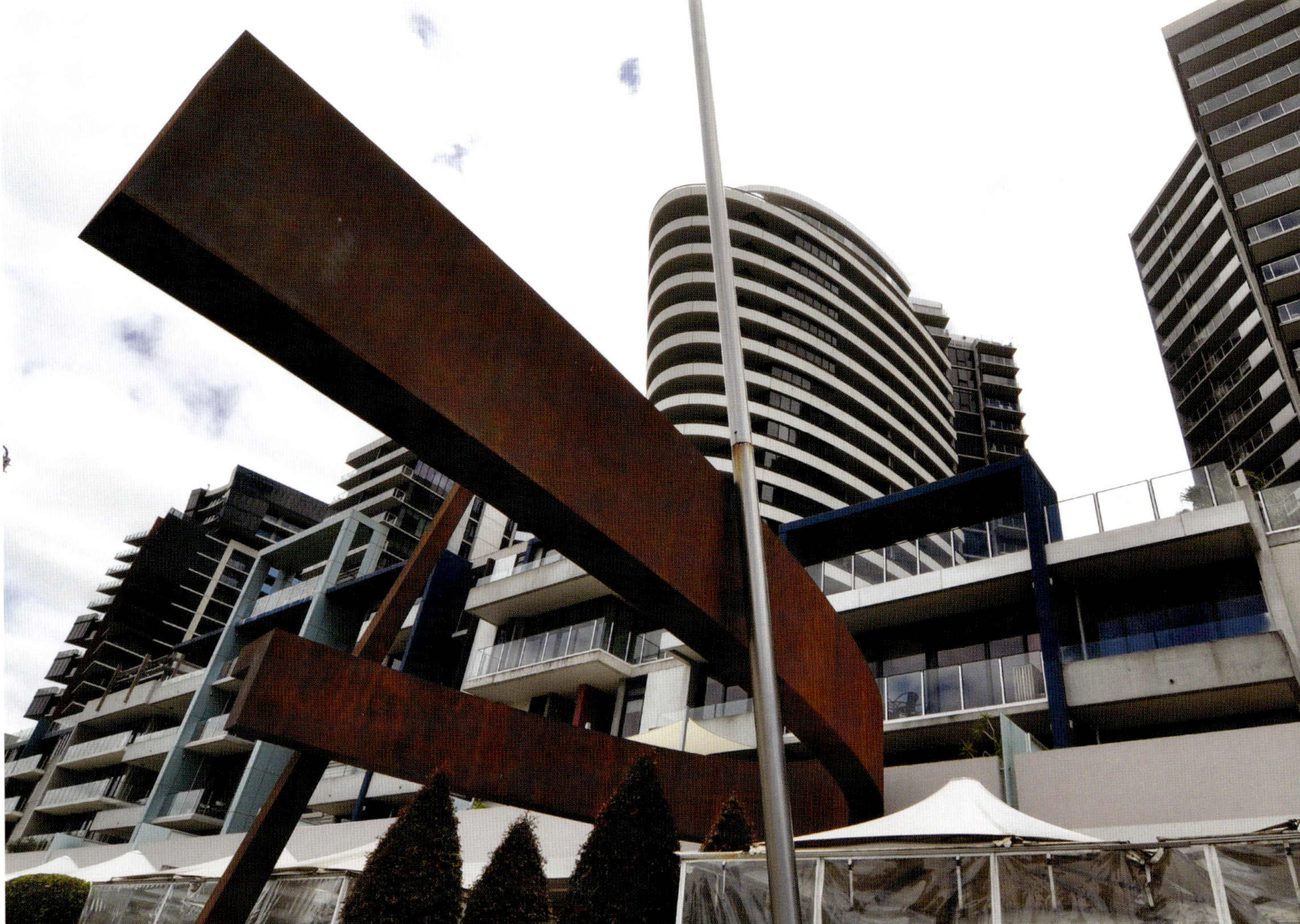

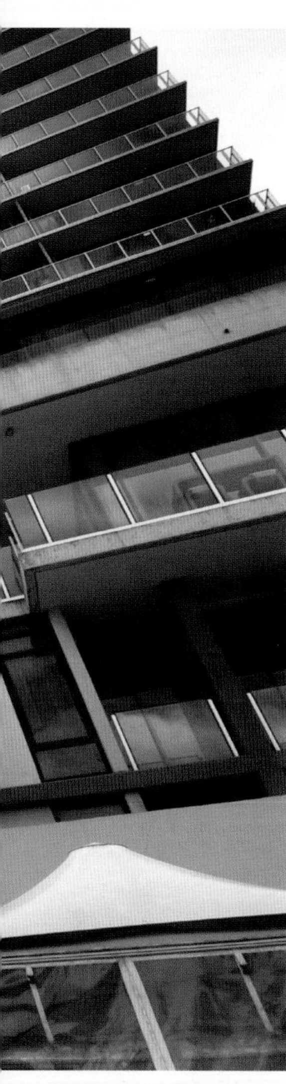

Docklands *continued...*

Bottom line: Come to the Docklands, experience Melbourne in a new way.

You will probably come back. You may even want to bunker down and stay!

It's growing fast and it's just down the road.

This beautiful waterfront precinct awaits you

Get into inner-city living mode.

Painting *NAB building and Dockland surrounds* [Previous page]
I was captivated by the NAB building in the Dockland context. Apparently, the design and colours showcase the importance of diversity, speaks of a bright future, while also respecting the areas port-container origins of the past. Brilliant concept. The existing colours certainly inspired this Painting the coloured foot path, the building facade, the jewel-blue sea each grabbed a hold of my attention to focus on this subject.

Photo *Docklands residential area, West of CBD* [Left]
There are many buildings with enormous flair, like this horse shoe design, which no doubt had a tonne of money spent on it. It will be very interesting to see how this city-port area appears overall in the coming decades as the city continues to grow.

Tip When shooting, the goal is often to bring out some exceptional distinguishing feature of the landscape. Highlighting unusual and striking shapes or features with a minimalist approach is my delight. The angle the shot is taken from can also create a certain dynamism.

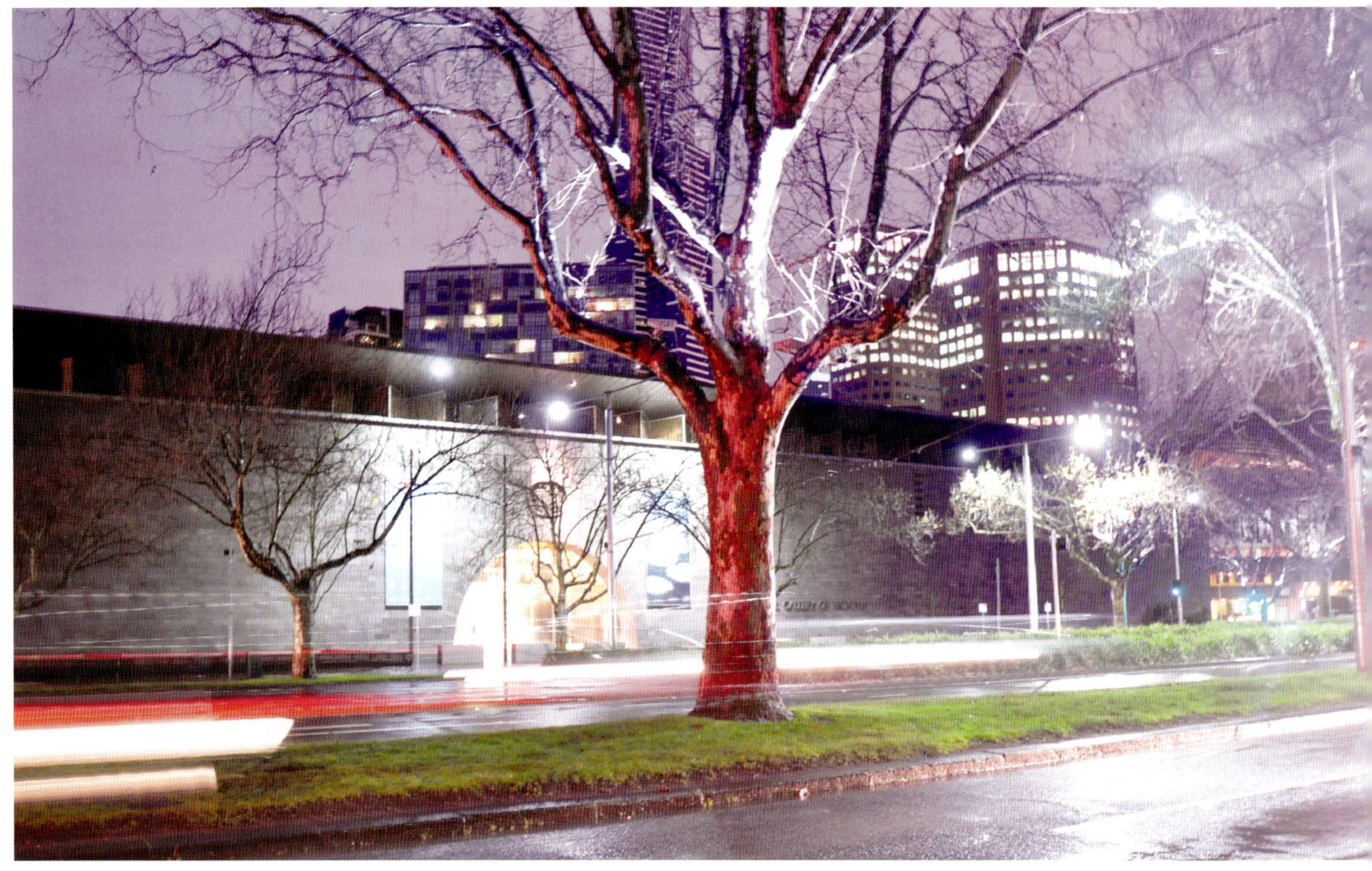

Photo *National Gallery of Victoria* [Above]
I took this photo just before dawn, in keeping with the poem's imagery. I got thoroughly soaked by the rain! The sense of mystique and adventure involved in getting the photo, and the vibrant purples captured in it, more than made up for the soaking.

National Gallery of Victoria

Melbourne art is promoted. Melbourne art is surely alive
People come daily to the NGV. It's as busy as a hive.
Rothko. Picasso. Amazingly not hard to find
On display for free. Come in off the street. Unwind.

Ever changing art, never the same from what has been.
Some take a glance at the Warhol's and the Pollock's and ask,
Is this progress, what do artists really mean?
For it appears there's no rhyme, no reason, so confusing it seems
But if you understand better the times they faced,
it helps you sympathise and better grasp the artist's dream.

The beauty of art is the way it lets you get what's inside out.
Creative concepts, experiences, feelings all assembled, permanent in front of you—
Art has a lot of clout.
Use twigs, bricks, cartons, paint—whatever you can find
But, the question I ask is how can art leave others feeling truly edified?

Truth is, every artist's work has beauty. There is beauty in it all.
For sure, artistic skill and eye catching composition are crucial
And yet, how is the art inspiring, creating meaning, hope, and joy?
Does it empower, touch your heart, makes you feel 10 feet tall?

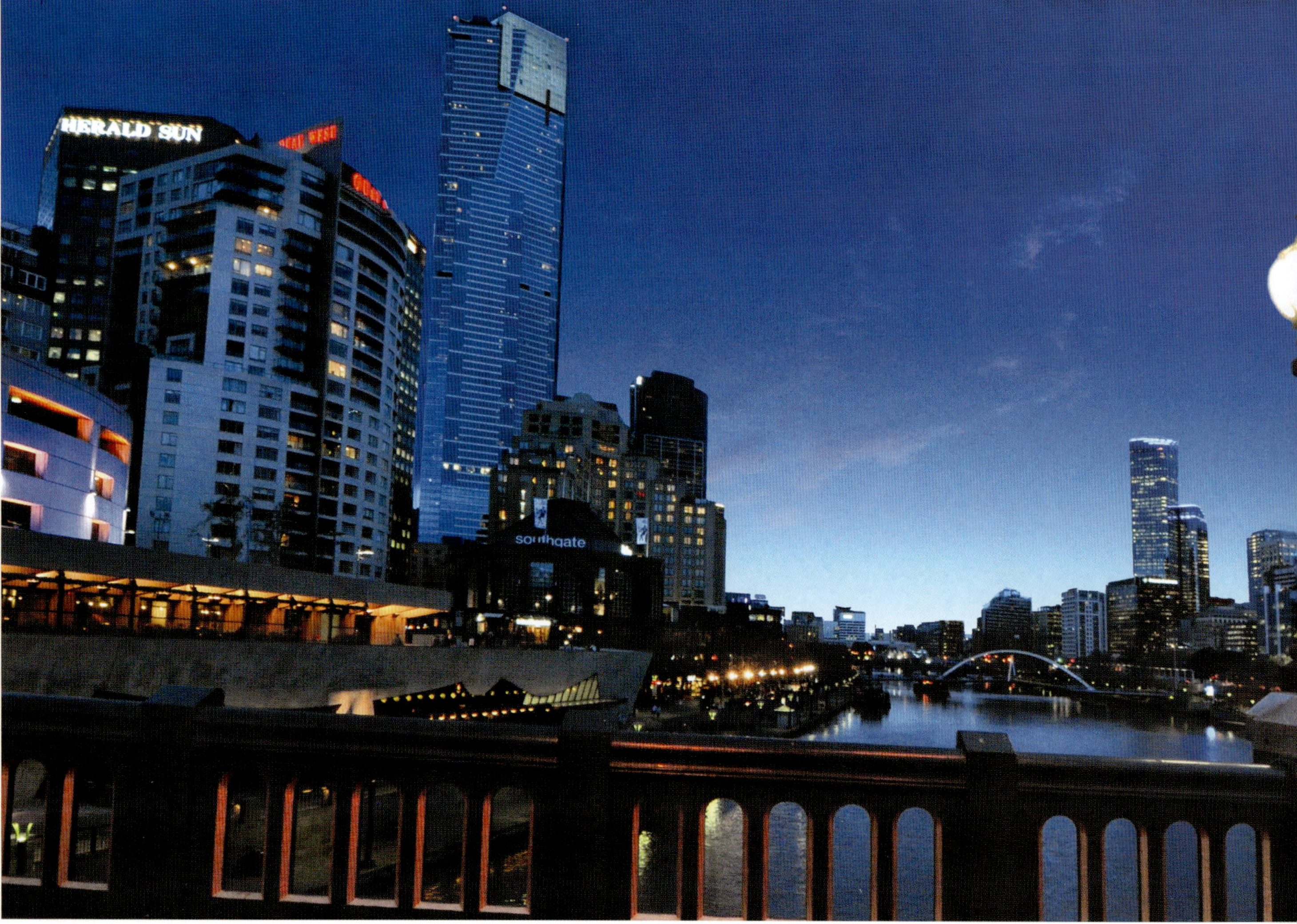
HERALD SUN
southgate

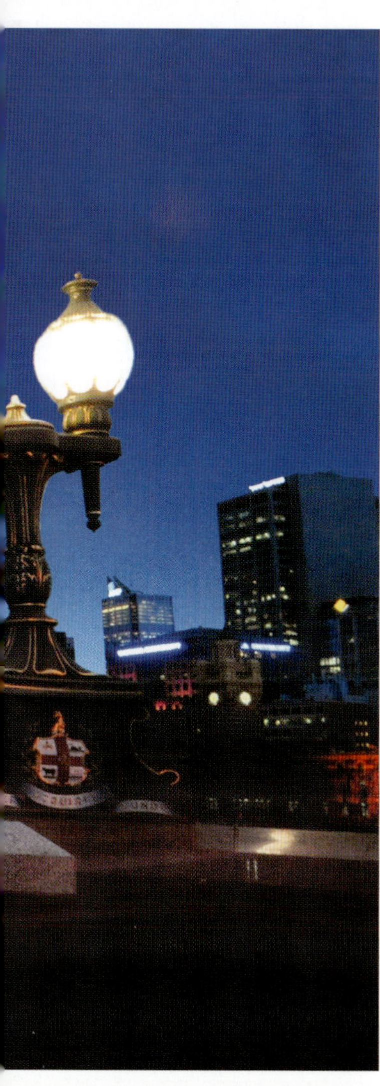

National Gallery of Victoria *continued...*

No denying that you have that creative streak in you.
Yet, you stare blankly at your canvas. Zero thought. You say, 'Oh me, Oh my!'
Instead let go, put brush to canvas; your creativity will surely multiply.

Keep going with your artistry; keep going as I did, because you know
Complete darkness is always followed by the vibrant brightness of dawn.
And maybe, who knows, you could become, the very next *Van Gogh*!

Photo — *Southbank Boulevard from the Yarra Bridge* [Left]
The idea was this shot was to portray ambiance and the lighting to portray why shoppers are drawn to this extravagant part of town, to support the poems intent.

Tip — Photos have moods too, like us. What emotion and feeling is being communicated through your photos?

Painting — *Cityscape, Southbank Boulevard* [Next page]
To be honest Van Gogh's Starry Night Cafe scene has always been a favourite of mine. It did inspire this work in part.

Tip — A great way to improve your design, writing, or entertaining skills is to expose yourself to a glut of good books and to people with like passion. We have amazing libraries in our home towns. Why not camp there sometimes? Everyone has some kind of unique angle to his or her work that we can learn from. Rub shoulders with others, especially those with differences so you are stretched in your perspective. If you do that, you can go from being more like a desert to becoming a fertile field, and in turn, a forest.

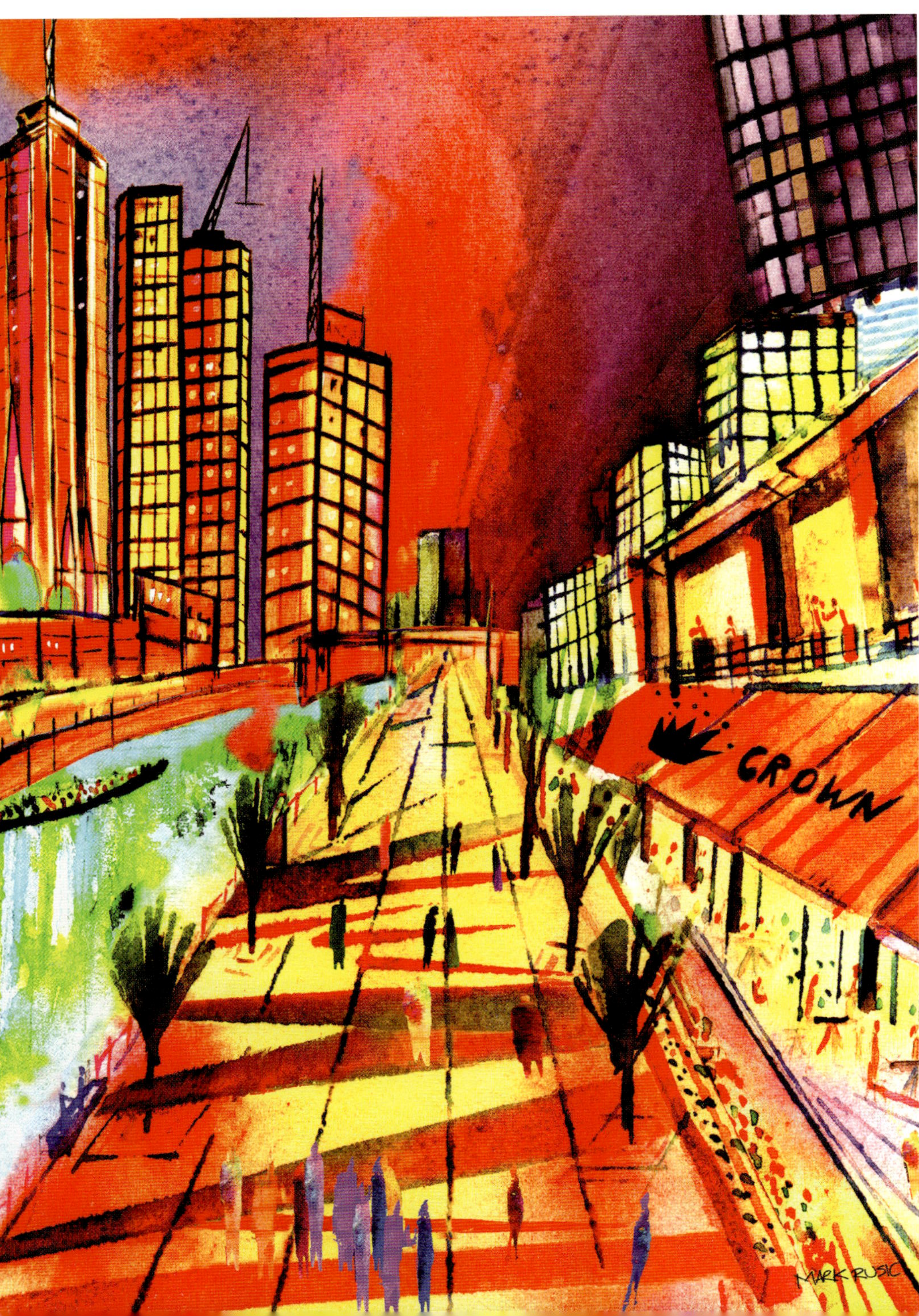
CROWN
MARK RUSIC

Southbank

Vibrant hub of activity, the Yarra Southgate strip.
Do I simply window shop, unwind, and let the credit card rip?
Great restaurants with city views, boutique and giftware shops, so much to see.
But, let's be honest about my finances; can I afford a spending spree?

Southbank. Entertainment facilities. A place of thrills.
But, it's hard to enjoy with pills to pop or if you can't pay the bills.
No worries mate, will just not do. How long can that last?
Sooner or later things explode; well before and not like, the fireworks
at Southbank's New Year's blast.

I saw a rich man I once knew. I pondered how he got rich.
Turns out he knew where every cent went. No holes in his wallet to stitch.
Creating wealth is a wisdom. Breaking sweat from hard work is okay.
Cause what counts is there's pizzas on the table; it's satisfying to pay.

So, be more careful with the heater. Switch off unused lights.
Cut back on unnecessary spending. More home cooked meals, less after-hour bites.
Cause the dollars you save today for tomorrow, could mean a better life.
Southbank is a place to enjoy. And it's best without squabbles over money,
and the associated strife!

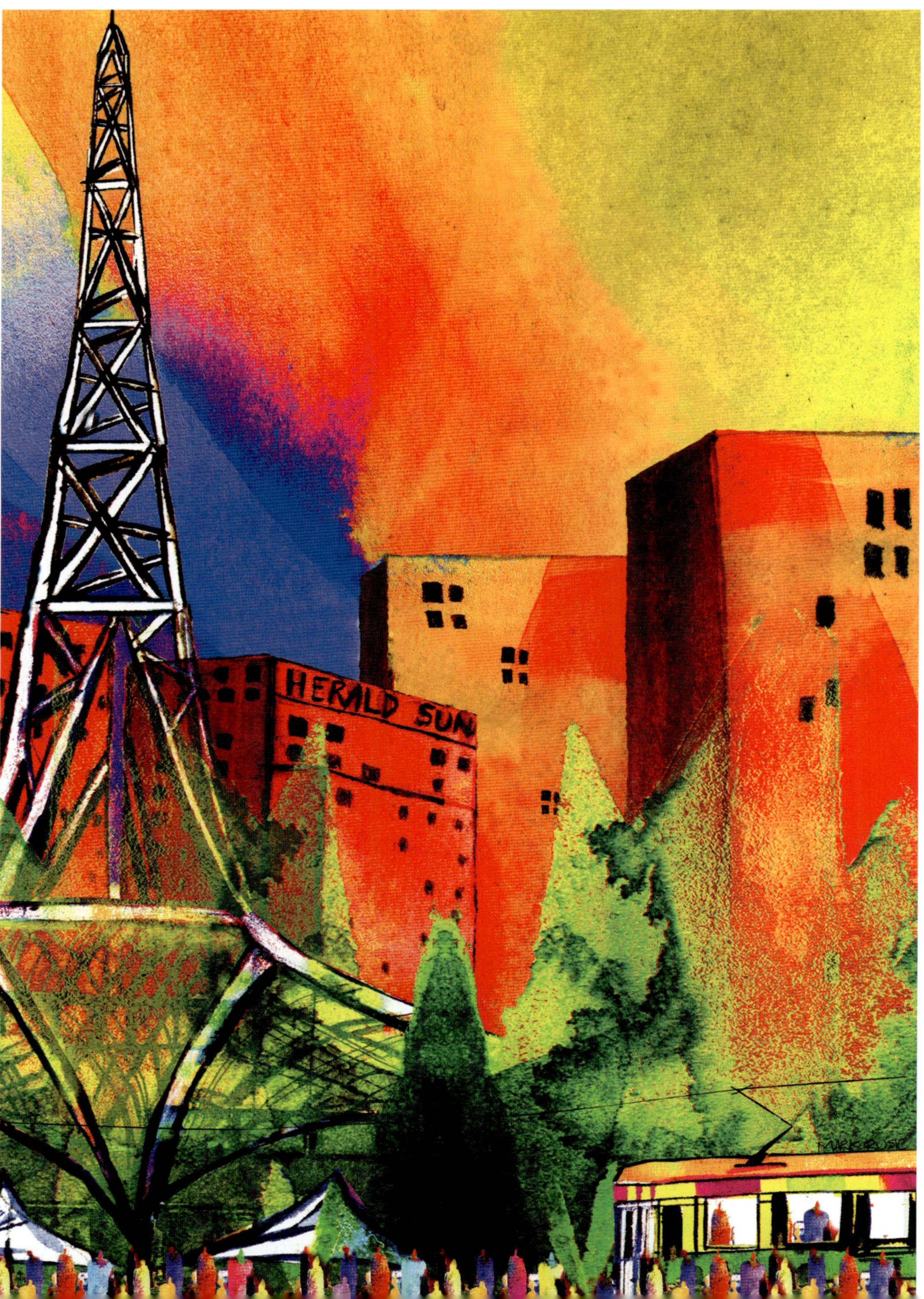
HERALD SUN

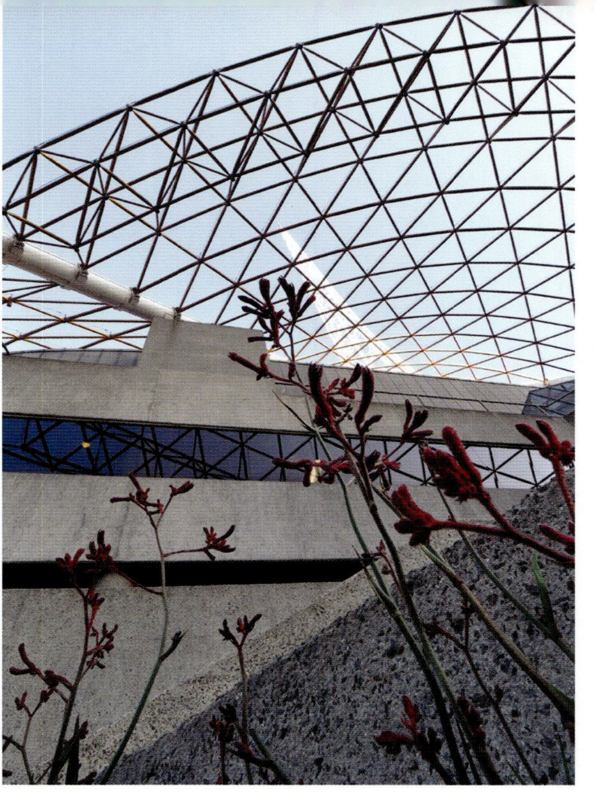

Painting *Arts Centre Melbourne* [Top]

This painting shows the Arts Centre in its glory. A key feature in this painting is the sky. When painting it, I had some intuitive sense I could bring these three colour streams together. My challenge: Wet into wet is hard to manage and I may get it wrong and lose my painting. Overall I was happy with the composition.

Tip

You have to cross the chicken-line to make art. In fact, to make that film, entertain those people or write that novel you need to cross that line. I think most of us don't because we too easily buy into our fears. We say in our hearts: Why waste my time? What if I mess up? What if people don't like me? Who am I?...

But, why not try a positive mindset. Take heart. We all know people who have said to us, we have something. So…what if it works? What if I actually live out my dream? I have an obligation to use my gift to make this world a better place! Cross the line, my friend. You have greatness within you. Cross it even as you read these words.

Pull out your laptop now. Start gathering your ideas....

Photo *Arts Centre Melbourne* [Above]

This shows a plant called Kangaroo Paw reaching up in the air, with the top of Arts Centre spire as if within reach. We all need to reach up for greater heights. In other words, it's good to pursue excellence and a life-vision that stretches you. That's because greatness is within us all; every single one of us. We certainly see that passion for excellence exemplified by those performing in the Melbourne Arts Centre.

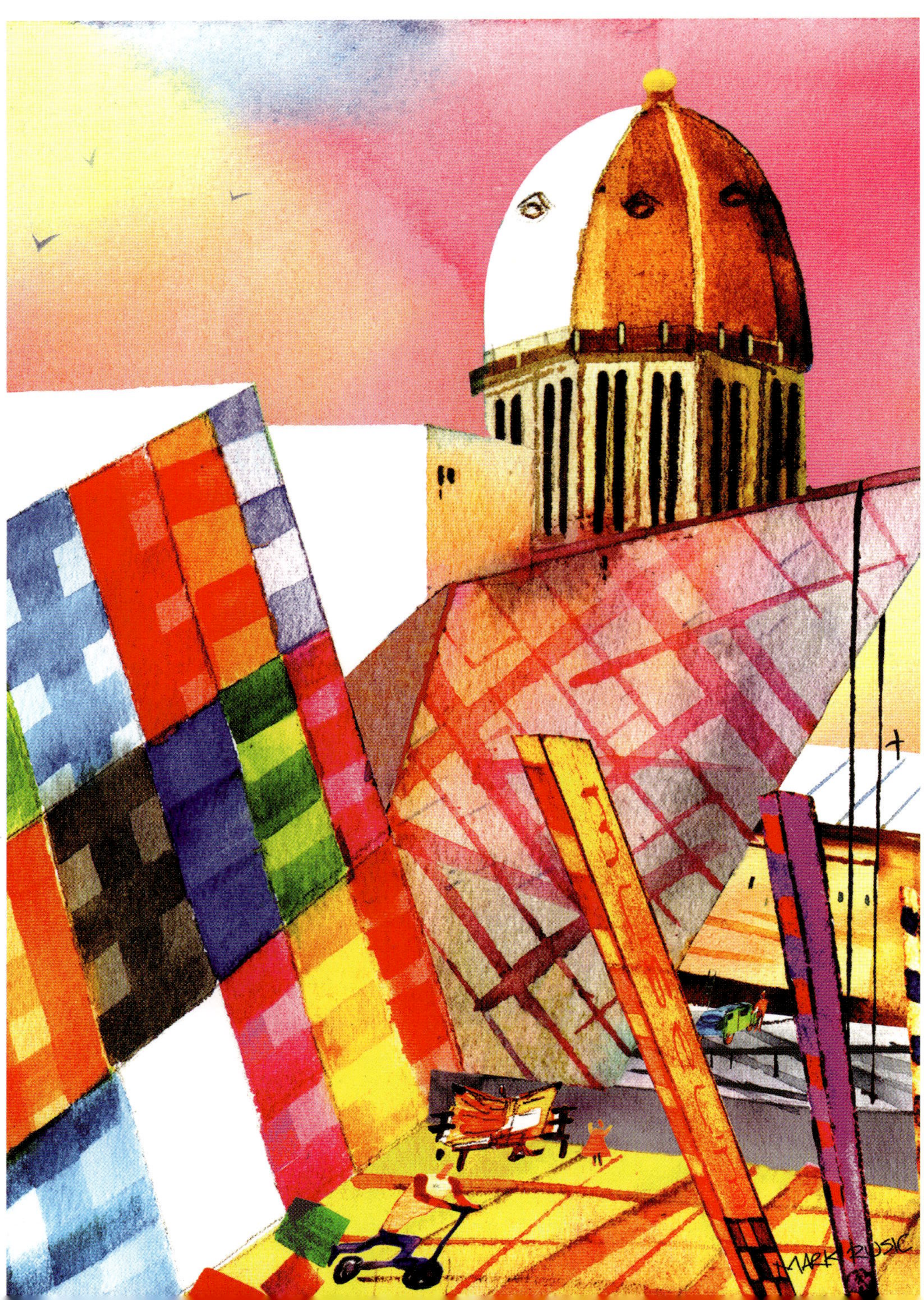
museum

Melbourne Museum

Walk through the Museum doors. Time is reversed, leap back in history.
To treasures of our distant past...

In exquisite presentation for all to see.
View the streets of Melbourne in the days of horse and carriage
and realise, I was not the first.
So many before me!
For each person has a story. Each person plays a part.
The great city we are today, began with a single step
Each one made a start.

Museums are more than a place of nostalgia for the past.
They are a springboard into our future
How society has developed. How we can make humanity last.
Be insightful, eager to learn, open your eyes to see
Or just enjoy. Your visit to the museum can be a wonderful time
with family, and also your great opportunity!

See, the question is will you be a history maker,
like those before us who were bold.
We can know how former migrants adapted, when the first person struck gold.
Learn from the movers and shakers, the city's sculptors, from days of old.
Be inspired by how our sports people won against the odds, how they broke out of the mould.

Knowing history is precious; it sheds light on how we used to live.
What we did right and wrong. Where we need to forgive.
History helps create the future; what is still undone?
Let it inspire you, and the world's history makers to
make history of your own and in fun!

So, if you're relaxing on the couch, or just watching TV
Maybe it's time to visit the Melbourne Museum, time
to spark into action, take that first step, take a leap
...May it not be your last. May you make history.

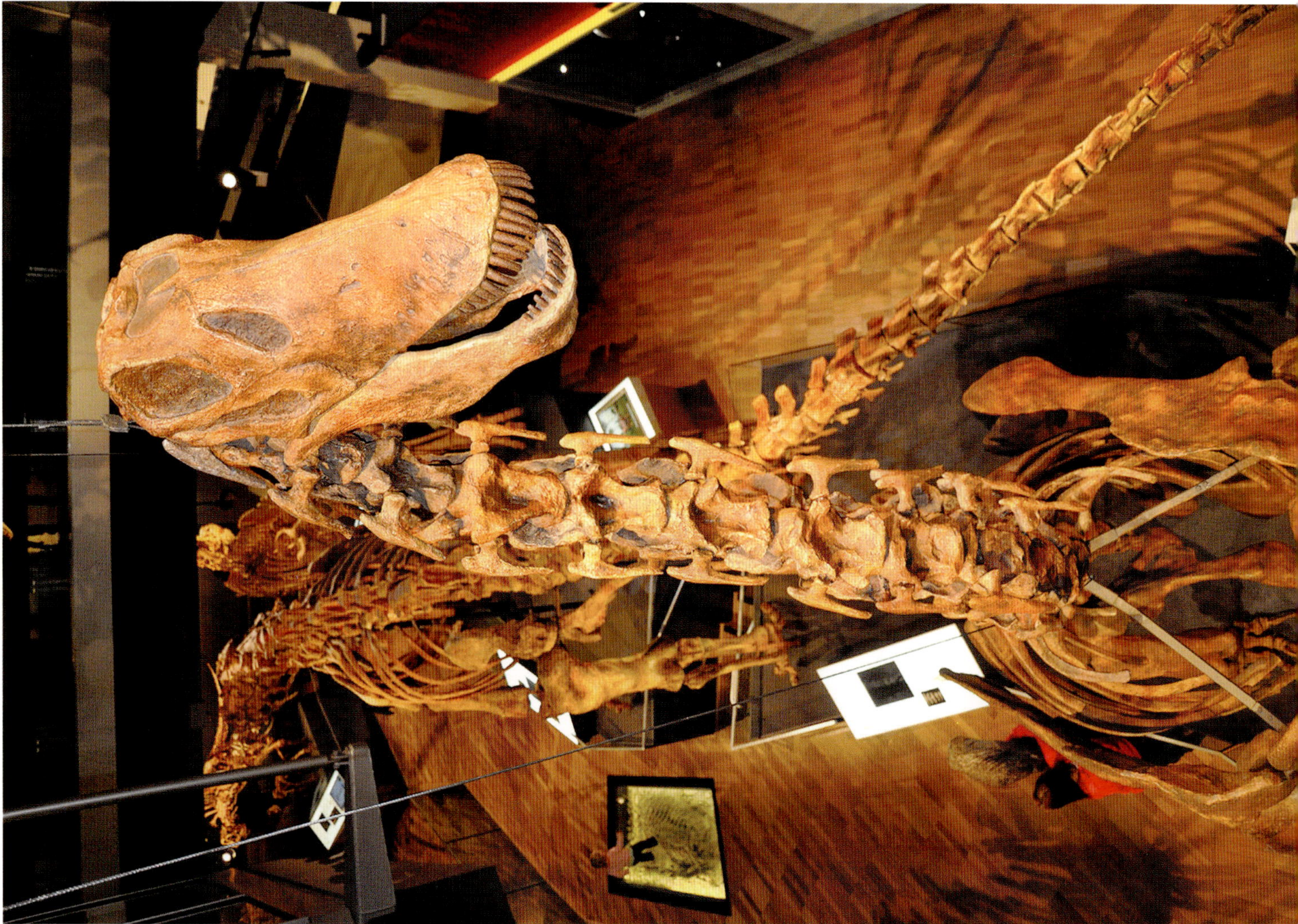

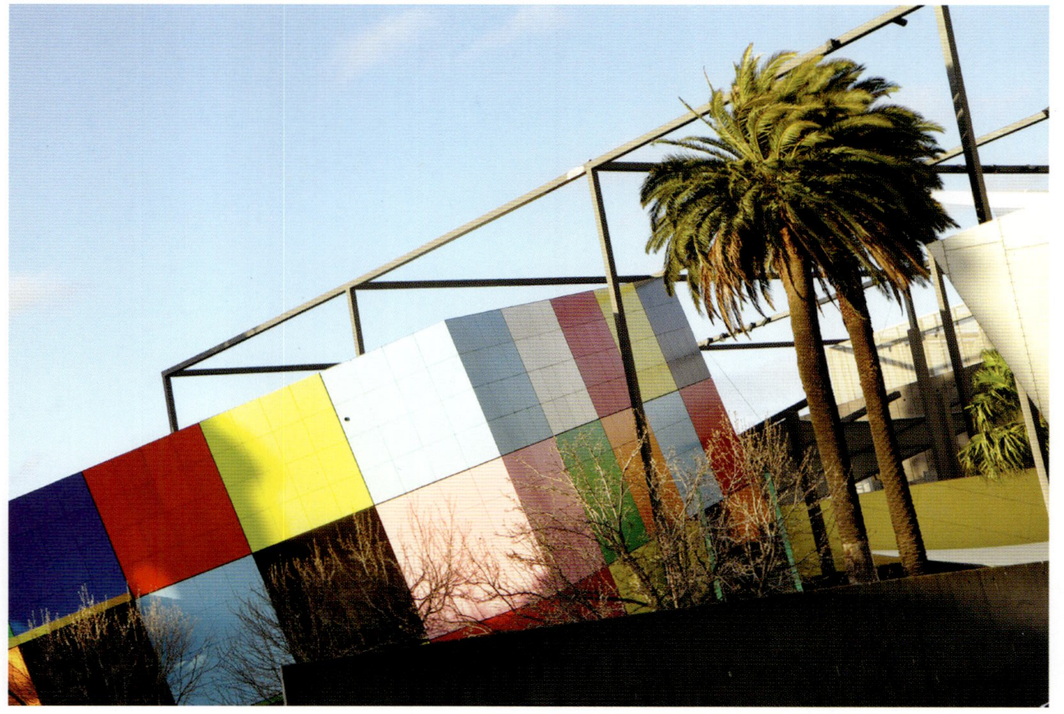

Painting — *Melbourne Museum* [Previous page]
With this particular angle of view I tried to juxtapose the old with the new; the stunning old exhibition building verses the highly contemporary finishes of the Melbourne Museum.

Photo — *Dinosaur Display, Melbourne Museum* [Top]
I call this photo: *The happy dinosaur*
I took well over fifty shots of the dinosaurs. The photo I chose to use here turned out to be the very last shot I took. I held the camera up flippantly not convinced it would be of use and fired at the dinosaur's mouth. As it turns out, it was clearly my most satisfying shot and unlike any of the standard literature on the Museum, which tends to highlight the Tyrannosaurus Rex instead.

Tip — Don't just go with the flow or follow the tide. Don't just focus on what others do; though be informed. (Others can be a great help.) Instead, focus on bringing out the best in your subject. Even take those shots you least expect to work; you may surprise yourself!

Photo — *The Big Box Forecourt Exterior, Melbourne Museum, Carlton Gardens* [Above]
I couldn't resist taking this shot of the cube. The colours and design are irresistible. Our Melbourne Museum is truly iconic with so many really unique and exciting features like this in its overall design.

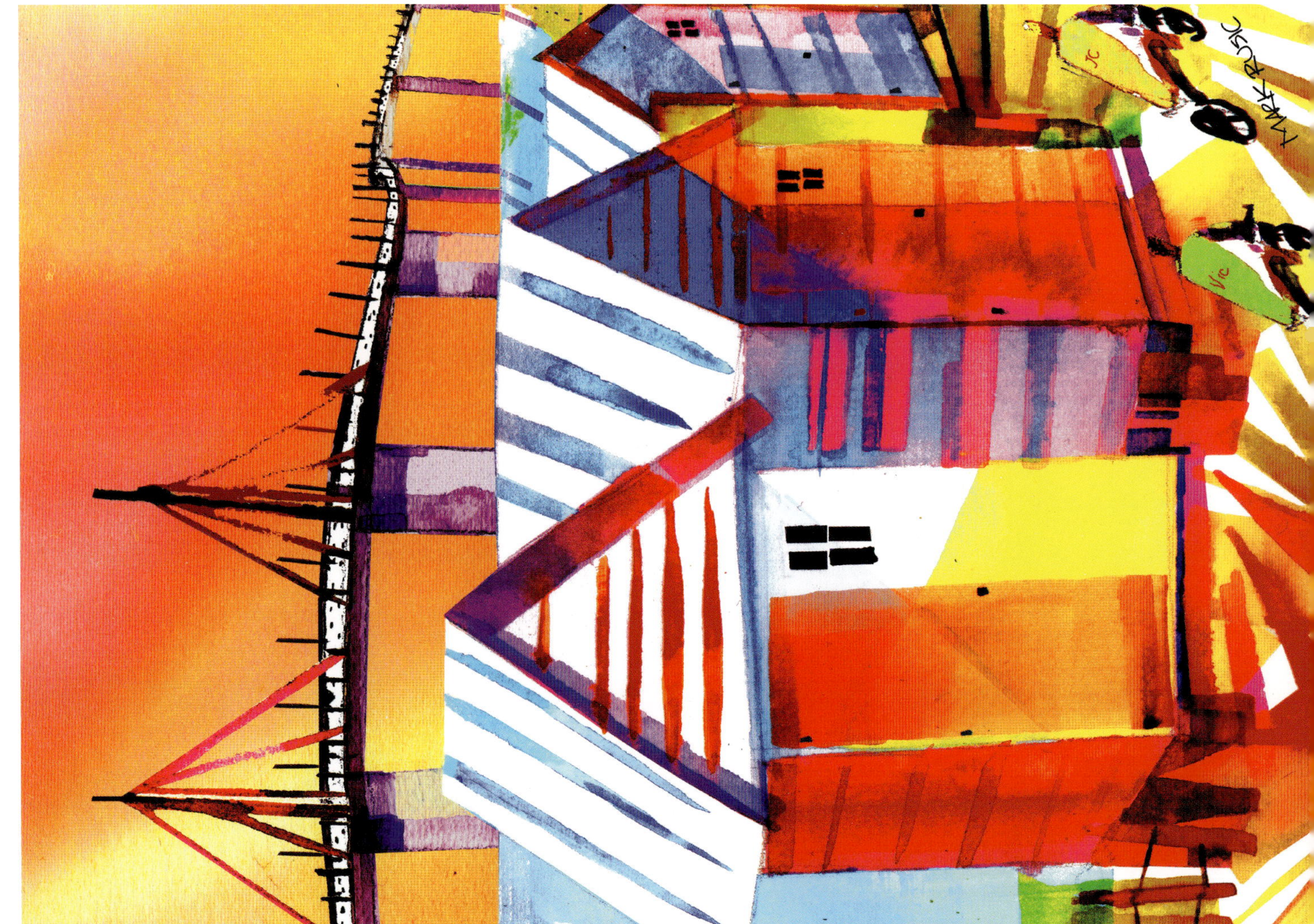

Brighton Bathing Boxes

Beautiful Brighton bathing boxes. Popular day trip down south
Like a shiny row of teeth, connected in a colourful line
Summer long their doors open, onto the ocean like a smiling mouth.
Owners recline comfortably beachside.
Across the shore, people strolling, swimming, jogging.
Like a lapping tongue, in and out goes the tide.

In the faint distance the West Gate Bridge, to the naked eye barely seen
I exercise my artistic licence and paint it overshadowing the houses.
Poor taste? Did I make the beautiful unclean?

Huge tidy up in order—Remove the bridge?...
The eyesores of life remain—despite our bubble and cocoon—around us
everywhere: poverty, pollution, some of us prisoners, pale and dying
Many others make us hurt and stare.
So liberating when men of estate and courage stand up
to make a difference in peoples' lives.
Reclining, smiling in your bathing box, with divine perspective
Knowing you are in position for such a time as this.
Destiny says, 'Give me that prize!'

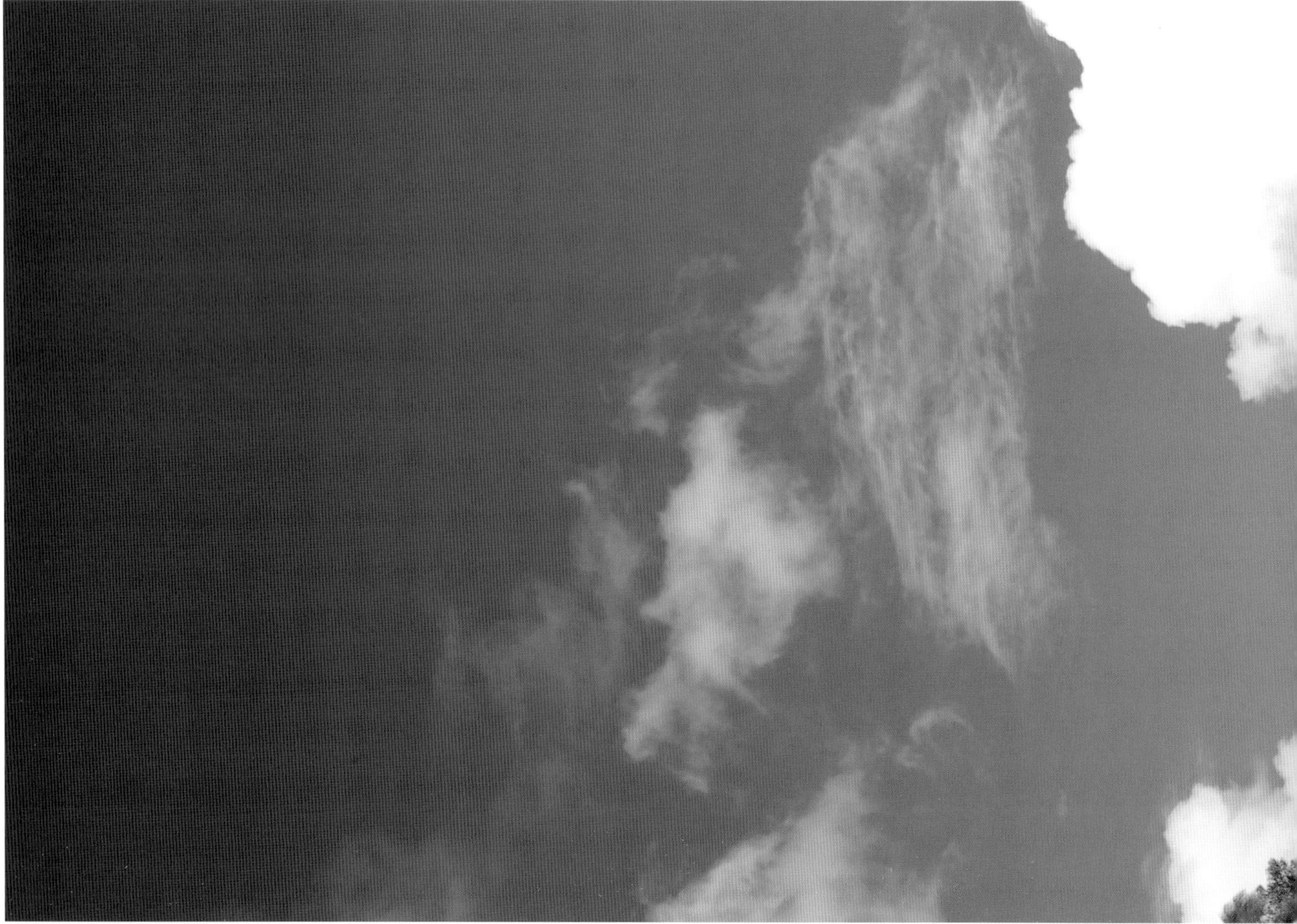

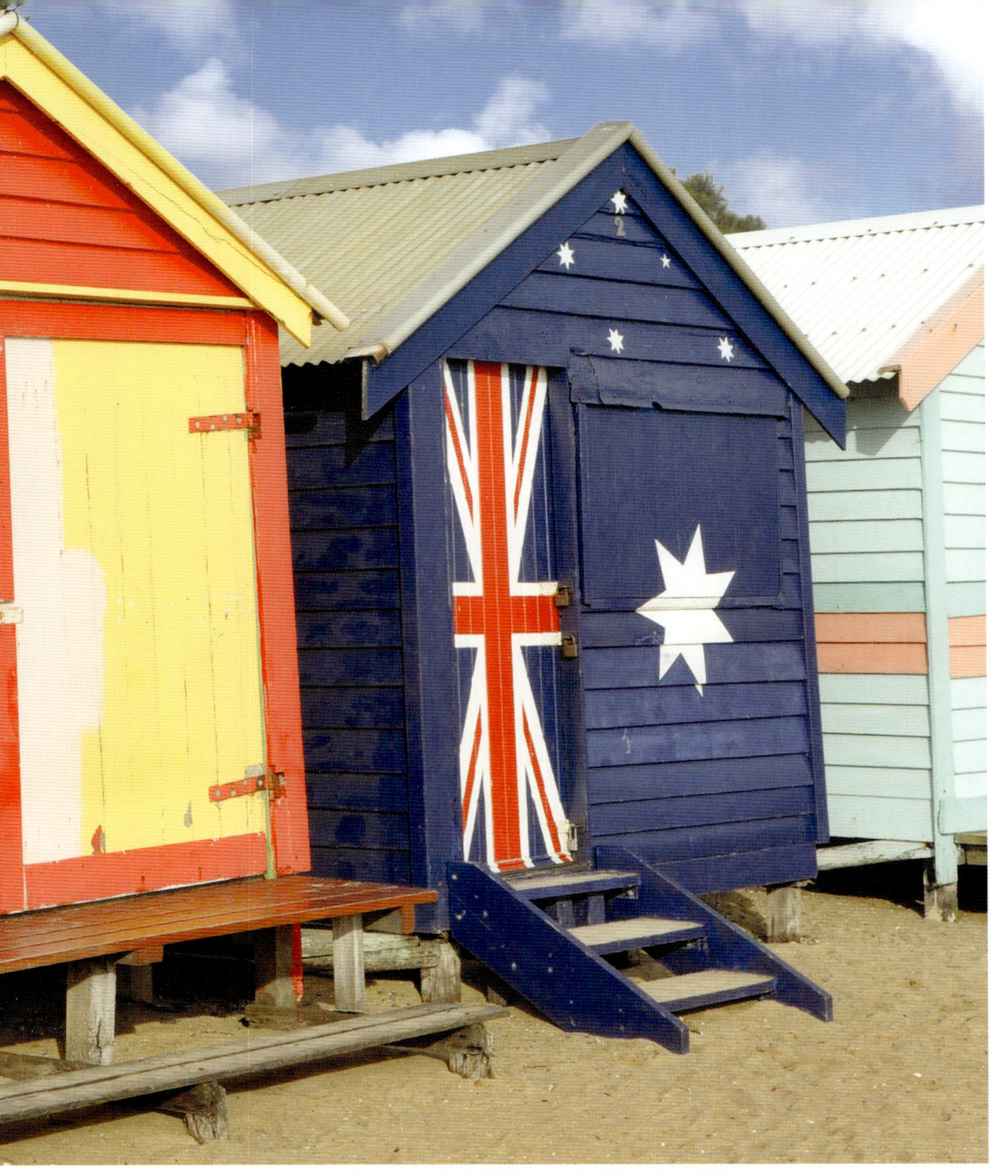

Painting — ***Bathing Boxes, Brighton*** [Previous page]
I used my artistic license to marry the West Gate Bridge with these lovely bathing boxes. It served a purpose. Oh, the fun of using artistic license; you can do as you please!

Photo — ***Bathing Boxes, Brighton*** [Above]
Here they are 'like a shiny row of teeth, connected in a colourful line.' Also, imagine the owner reclining in his bathing box, laughing, chuckling, pondering his dream for the betterment of humanity and lives touched. The dominance of the lovely white clouds and blue sky above the bathing boxes symbolises this divine perspective.

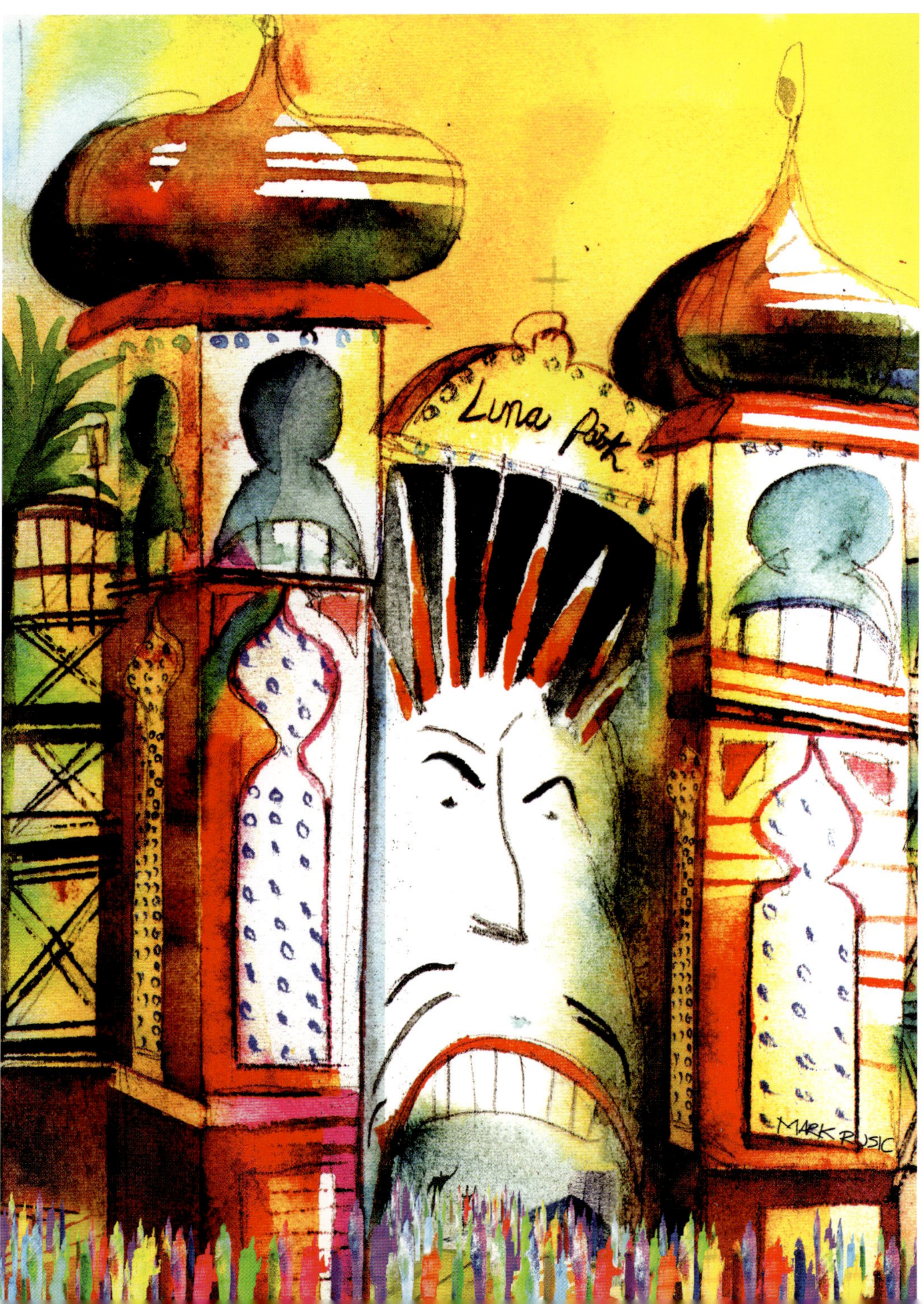
Luna Park
MARK RUSIC

Luna Park

To whom it may concern:

A search for true happiness. A search for fun.
Maybe you've tried career, relationships, drugs and alcohol, video games—
everything under the sun? And yet the more you've tried, the more
your heart thirsts and shrinks. Why is there a hole?
A few good laughs at the fun park and Still—
your life is not feeling great. It feels like you are on the brink.

A riddle:

Just for fun, just for fun. Whatever goes, under the sun

Whatever goes, whatever goes, but what is right? People say, *who knows?*

Eat them up, eat them up. Fear upon us, we all shut up

Monday blues, down in the dumps. Cynicism reigns.
Suddenly the penny drops. Now there is peace inside
the pain Stops!

Just for fun, just for fun. Wild sense of satisfaction. Enjoying it all from above the sun.

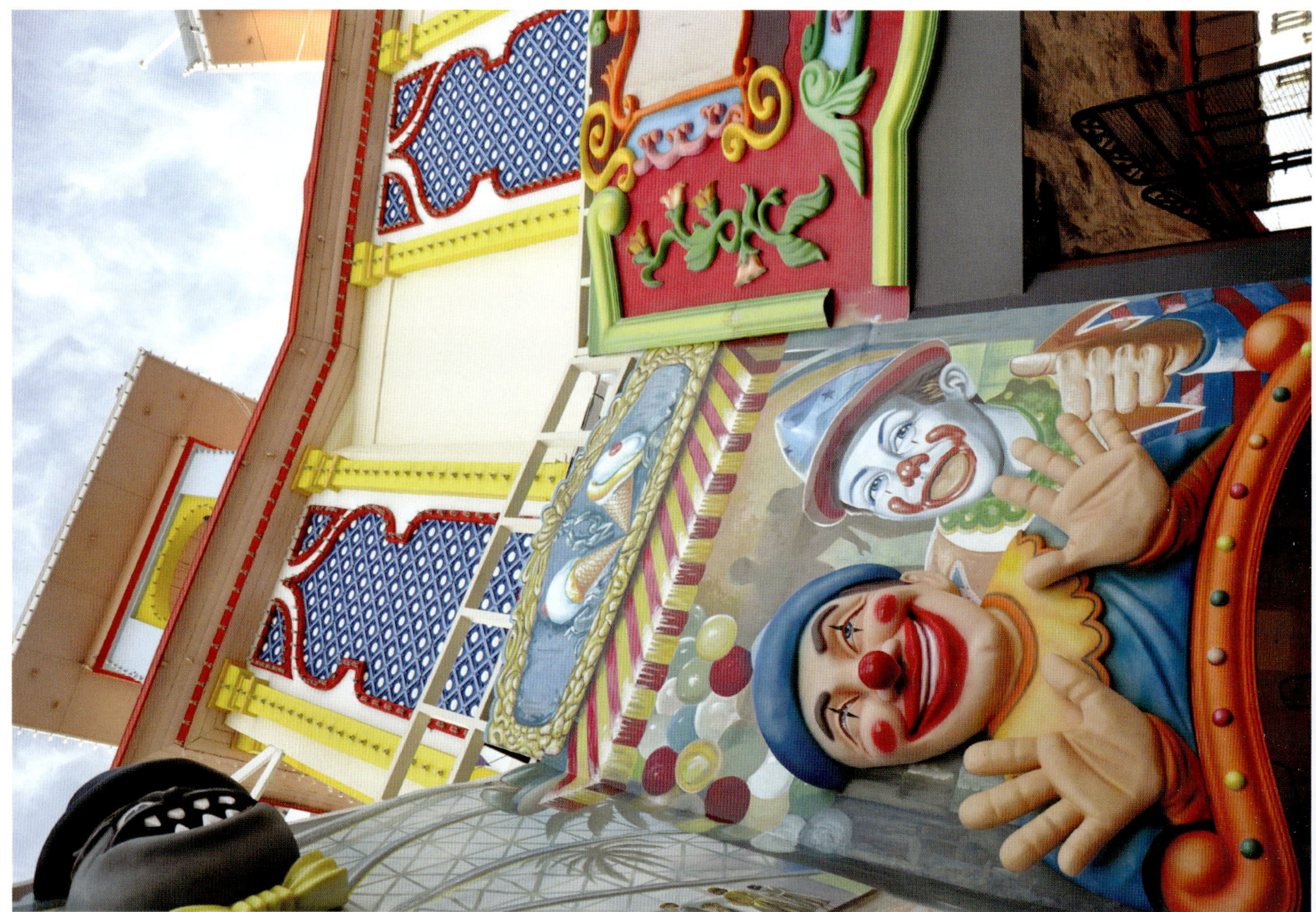

Painting *Luna Park entrance, St Kilda* [Previous page]

I made the face a little more hideous to portray Luna Park figuratively 'eating people up' so it relates to the meaning of the poem. Keeping the painting's subject balanced, with yellow as the dominant colour, was the challenge. I was happy with the outcome.

Photo *Wall art inside Luna Park grounds* [Above]

This is one amazing section of art and wall decoration found only at Luna Park. Can you see how these clowns representing 'just for fun' idea are 'under the sun?' The eye starts and begins with the clowns and makes its way up to the sky. I believe there is profound meaning reflected in this photo which perfectly works together with the poem and painting in this art-unison.

Tip

Art is about beauty. The beauty of any artwork is reflected in its eye catching composition, originality and skill. Also, I believe that the beauty of an artwork is greatly amplified when the art also communicates a depth and substance of meaning that encourages some kind of positive social outlook and gives hope.

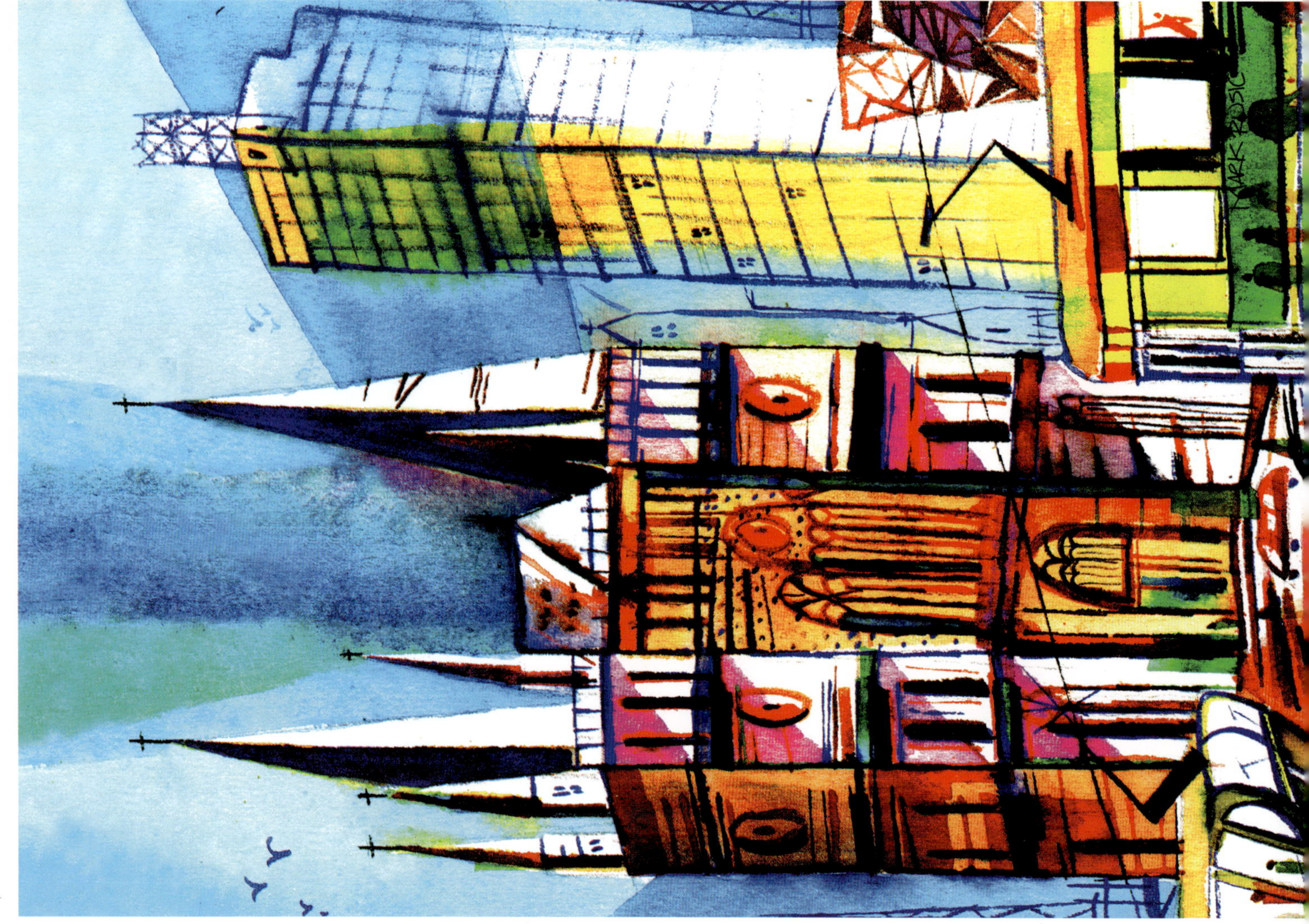

St Paul's Cathedral

Where do you turn and where do you go
When friends don't seem to care and family doesn't want to know
When life's pressures mount up, promises fall through
When you're a number in the system, or people want to sue.

People will tell you problems are a part of life.
Life wasn't meant to be easy. It's normal to have strife.
You'll get over it. It will be fine.
But some people just can't cease to whine.

St Paul's is where many a soul comes to pray.
Especially when hurting, in trouble or disarray.
A place of peace and a place to shed your tears,
To get through your darkest valley and overcome your deepest fears.

St Paul's itself, extraordinary, masterful in design,
Huge arches and spires, glorious light through leadlight shines
Man's best effort to help us focus on the One above.
And yet it's totally all by amazing grace that we can know His love.

Human beings are fallible. At times what happens in our world is cruel.
But One stands out, matchless with perfect justice and love
To seek Him we are no fool.
Men were led by following a star, now countless numbers claim to see
what the Good Book is really saying…
Is there truly someone out there for you and me?

Many voices are calling. Many paths we can take.
Many directions to pursue. What decision will you make?
Enter the doors with the glorious light. Trade your sin and burden with His
free gift of righteousness
Christ knocks on the door of your heart.
Open. Strife gone. Your life can have a brand new start!

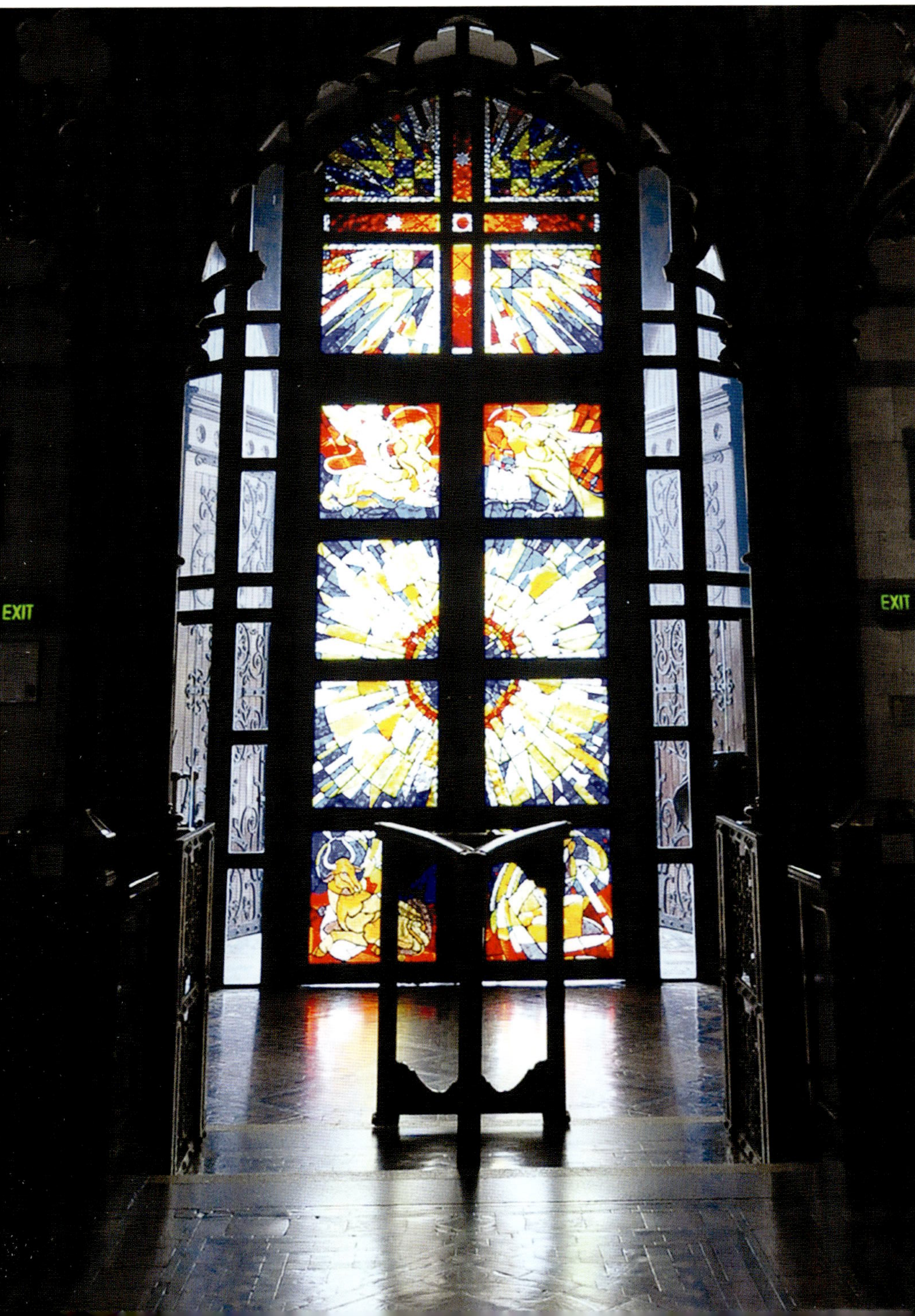
EXIT
EXIT

Painting

St Paul's Cathedral [Previous page]

Blue is a spiritual colour. I used lots of it here. What I love is how it's being interrupted by certain irregular layers of more blue. This contrast creates dynamism. The house of God is a living house, made up of lively stones.

Photo

Main entrance door, St Paul's Cathedral [Above]

I mentioned that the door is always open. I tried to use the leadlight to make the entry as inviting as possible. Christ welcomes us no matter what state we are in.

A DEDICATION (An extension from the Flinders Street Poem, page 10-11)

Family is a vital part of life. I had to learn to honour my parents, to practically see my family life improve. Here is an additional stanza in dedication to my wonderful father and mother:

I love my family and my home.
I loved them too much to stay away. But, I almost accepted an unhealthy norm—
Of little-to-no communication; letting things fray.
A time came when I knew I needed to change. I needed to accept the family call.
I discovered that everyone in my family wanted the same.
So I got back on those tracks. And down came all the walls!

Mark Rusic was born in Melbourne, Australia. He is a self-taught artist, poet and photographer. From an early age, Mark showed signs of having some unique artistic ability. However, Mark buried down his passion for the arts due to life disappoints and instead studied engineering at university. One day, through a deeply personal, heavenly God-encounter, his passion was revived and the creative side came out of 'cold storage'. The chip on his shoulder was taken away. Colour, life-meaning and hope blossomed from that time on. While it was a rocky start finding his greater potential, he persevered. Then, exciting things began to happen. A customer bought a dozen of his paintings and told him the images and colours helped him to overcome his depression; Mark knew then he was on to something!

Mark progressed to selling art in local Melbourne markets. From here his childhood passion for poetry and photography was rekindled. So, over time Mark made a journey back to being creative and in doing so, he found himself! One thing that inspires him to keep creating is hearing what people actually feel about his artistry. Mark has included some testimonials from buyers of his work from Australia and across the globe.

"I loved the colours and imagination. It's really unique and you don't see this sort of stuff anywhere." **(Melbourne)**

"I've been holidaying in Melbourne for 8 months and have been waiting for a piece of artwork to jump out at me. I've finally found it. Thanks so much." **(Canada)**

"These pictures evoke an endless number of ever enjoyable emotions and are priceless visual euphoria." **(Melbourne)**

"Captured my imagination. Captures Melbourne. I had to turn back and look again. Look forward to hanging it in my home in Canada." **(Canada)**

"Beautiful artwork. I can't wait to get to my new place so I can put this up. Captures the best of Australia." **(US)**

"It's amazing how you captured the 'vibe' of St Kida. Will take this to my family in Venezuela." **(Venezuela)**

"The colours, visual style and uniqueness drew me in and I was hooked. Thanks for a unique souvenir." **(UK)**

"Brings out such beautiful memories from beach holidays in my childhood-the colours & the feeling in these are so powerful & lovely!" **(Melbourne)**

"Eye catching colours, an inspiration. Love your work. Am taking home our memories of Melbourne." **(NSW, Australia)**

"Love your art! Have never seen a painting that I'd like to have in my room till I met you. Keep on going!" **(Austria)**

"Striking colours, look forward to my friend admiring them when I get home to Scotland. They will remind me of my wonderful holiday in Australia." **(Scotland)**

Any comments or testimonials, or orders for prints of the artwork & photography-
Email to givejoydesigns@gmail.com